M000207922

LLEWELLYN'S
Tarot
Reader
2005

Featuring

Ruth Ann and Wald Amberstone, Nina Lee Braden,
Bonnie Cehovet, Joan Cole, Elizabeth Genco,
Mary K. Greer, Elizabeth Hazel, Christine Jette,
Corrine Kenner, Mark McElroy, Errol McLendon,
Kevin Quigley, Janina Renée, Valerie Sim, Thalassa,
James Wells, Diane Wilkes, and Winter Wren

Editing/Design by K. M. Brielmaier
Cover Design by Kevin R. Brown
Interior Art by Nyease Somerset
Art Direction by Lynne Menturweck

Table of Contents

The Fool: Tools for the Journey

The Magician: Practical Applications

✳ ☆ ✳ ☆ ✳ ☆ ✳ ☆ ✳ ☆ ✳ ☆ ✳ ☆ ✳

The Wheel of Fortune: 2005 Almanac

The Hermit: For Further Study

Judgment: Deck Reviews

The World: Spreads

✴ ☆ ✴ ☆ ✴ ☆ ✴ ☆ ✴ ☆ ✴ ☆ ✴ ☆ ✴

About the Authors

Ruth Ann and Wald Amberstone are well-known in the tarot community as highly creative and original teachers. They are founders of the Tarot School and authors of *The Tarot School Correspondence Course* and *Tarot Tips: 78 Practical Techniques to Enhance Your Reading Skills*. They are also the creators of the Readers Studio, an annual national conference for tarot professionals.

Nina Lee Braden, the author of *Tarot for Self Discovery*, lives with her husband Mike Willis in Tennessee. She and her husband met when he came to a tarot class that she was teaching. When she is not teaching, reading, editing, or writing, Nina Lee enjoys playing games on her computer and going to movies.

Bonnie Cehovet is a tarot master, a professional tarot reader with over ten years of experience, a reiki master/teacher, and a writer. She has served in various capacities with the American Tarot Association, including secretary on the ATA Board. She is co-founder of the World Tarot Network and Director of Certification for the American Board For Tarot Certification. She currently has columns appearing in the World Tarot Network newsletter ("Stray Thoughts From Bonnie's Corner") and on the Meta Arts e-magazine site ("Gateway To Tarot"). She is editor of her own monthly newsletter, *Gateway To Tarot*.

Joan Cole first encountered a tarot deck the summer before she went to college, where she earned a bachelor's degree in anthropology and a master's degree in accountancy. Mundanely, she worked as an information technologist for ten years before becoming a full-time stay-at-home mom. Although she has been a member of various ritual groups over the years, and has formed several short-lived ones, tarot has been her main focus over the last twenty years, providing the structure for study in various flavors and eras of occultism. She has a very strong interest in occult history and iconography, and a passion for puzzling out underlying structures and patterns in decks.

Elizabeth Genco is a systems engineer, fiddle player, tarot enthusiast, and writer, though not necessarily in that order. Her online magazine, PLATFORM, is about her experiences as a busker in the New York City subways. She divides her time between New York City and Los Angeles.

Mary K. Greer is an author and teacher specializing in methods of self-exploration and transformation. She is featured at tarot conferences and symposia in the United States and abroad. Active in several tarot associations and internet discussion groups, she teaches and writes for the women's and Pagan communities, and is an Arch-Priestess/Hierophant in the Fellowship of Isis. Tools and Rites of Transformation (T.A.R.O.T.) is a learning center founded and directed by Mary for the study of divination, women's mysteries, and the transformative arts. Her books include *Understanding the Tarot Court* with Tom Tadfor Little, *The Complete Book of Tarot Reversals, Tarot for Your Self: A Workbook for Personal Transformation, The Essence of Magic: Tarot, Ritual, and Aromatherapy, Tarot Mirrors: Reflections of Personal Meaning,* and *Tarot Constellations: Patterns of Personal Destiny*.

Elizabeth Hazel has had a lifelong passion for tarot and astrology. She authored *The Tarot Decoded* and continues to develop innovative techniques for blending the stars and cards with mythology, mantra, art, and music. Liz resides in Toledo, Ohio.

Christine Jette is a registered nurse and holds a bachelor of arts degree in psychology. She is the author of *Tarot Shadow Work, Tarot for the Healing Heart, Tarot for All Seasons,* and *Professional Tarot*. She lives with her husband and three cats.

Corrine Kenner is a certified tarot master and the mother of three girls who range in age from toddler to teen. She is the author of Llewellyn's *Tarot for Romance*.

Mark McElroy is the author of *Putting the Tarot to Work*, a book on visual brainstorming for business, and *Putting the Tarot to Bed*, the brainstorming book for love, sex, and relationships.

Errol McLendon, CTI, is a tarot reader, writer, and teacher in the Chicago area where he lives with his wife, Wendye, and his dogchild, Morgan. Errol began reading cards in 1997 after a particularly unprofessional reading in New Orleans prompted him to buy his first deck to "find out what all this stuff is about." He continues to find out every day. As TarotGuy, Errol promotes tarot as "practical, not mystical." In addition to serving as the vice president of education for the American Tarot Association, Errol currently reads on two free-reading networks, regularly teaches a fifteen-week master class in Chicago, and mentors numerous students over the Internet.

Kevin Quigley has been reading and studying tarot for more than ten years. His spiritual practice can be described as being both eclectic and pragmatic. He employs a variety of different perspectives to compare, contrast, conflict, and support each other.

Janina Renée is a scholar of material culture, folklore, mythology, ancient religion, psychology, medical anthropology, history, and literature. She is also the author of *Tarot Spells*, *Playful Magic*, *Tarot: Your Everyday Guide*, *Tarot for a New Generation*, and *By Candlelight: Rites for Celebration, Blessing, and Prayer*.

Valerie Sim is the listowner of the popular tarot e-mail list "Comparative Tarot." Her first book, *Tarot Outside the Box*, is due out in 2004, and she is now at work on her second book, *Shamanic Tarot*. She wrote the "little white book" for the recently published *Comparative Tarot Deck* and is the editor for both *Tarot Reflections* and the *ATA Quarterly*.

Thalassa is the producer of the San Francisco Bay Area Tarot Symposium (SF BATS), founder of Daughters of Divination (DOD), and publisher of *The Belfry* (purveyor of the finest divinatory journalism in the Western world). She reads, teaches, and produces divination-inspired events in both northern and southern California. She has been working with tarot, divination, and magic for more than thirty-six years, and wonders if she's ever going to see more than the shapely ankles of the Divine. She lives in San Francisco with a collection of swords, an assortment of historical costumes, too many books, and a tribe of semi-feral dustbunnies—not to mention more tarot decks than one can safely shake a stick at.

James Wells is a Toronto-based tarot consultant, reiki master, ritual weaver, and workshop facilitator. He provides sacred time and space for insight, healing, and constructive feedback. James is a member of the International Tarot Society, the Daughters of Divination, and the Inner Order of the Sapphire Pentacle. He is a sought-after presenter on tarot, ritual, divination, and personal growth.

Diane Wilkes is a tarot author and teacher who has been reading cards for over thirty years. She is the author of the *Storyteller Tarot* and the forthcoming *Jane Austen Tarot*, which will be published by Lo Scarabeo in 2005. A certified tarot grand master, Diane is also the webmistress of Tarot Passages, a comprehensive and popular Internet site devoted primarily to tarot.

Winter Wren is a tarot professional, certified as both tarot master and tarot educator, with over twenty years of experience in the discipline. She sits as executive vice president with the American Board for Tarot Certification and is a member of both the American Tarot Association and the International Tarot Society. She publishes a weekly tarot meditation list through her Tarot Box website. When not reading tarot, she is often writing about tarot. Wren makes her home in central Illinois.

The Fool

Tools for the Journey

IL MATTO · LE FOU · 0 · THE FOOL · EL LOCO · DER NARR · DE DWAAS

The Birth of the Tarot

by Mary K. Greer

D espite popular myths of tarot's origin in Egypt or Morocco or with the heretic Cathars or Templars, and of its spread by Gypsies, all historical evidence suggests that tarot cards were created between 1420 and 1440 in northern Italy, probably Milan or Ferrara. The symbolism is Christian and the images common in the late Middle Ages and early Renaissance.

The Origin of Playing Cards

Playing cards appeared in Europe at least fifty years earlier, having originated in China by at least the tenth century. The concept was appropriated by the Seljuk conquerers from Kazakhstan and, in turn, by the Mongol rulers Genghis and Kublai Khan. Its development followed the circuitous invasion and trade routes from China through Persia (with a separate link into India) to Mamlûk Egypt before arriving in Spain (or southern Italy) no later than the 1370s. It is from Catalonia that we have the earliest European records of playing cards and cardmakers. Aided by the recently developed papermaking and woodblock printing techniques, cards soon appeared all over Europe, where they were adapted to many new forms.

Playing cards were originally called *naypes* or *naibi*, a name that most likely derives from an Arabic term, *na'ib*, which was inscribed on two of the Mamlûk court or face cards. By 1400 the Mamlûks had a card deck consisting of fifty-two cards with suits of Swords, Polo Sticks, Cups, and Coins, numbered one through ten, plus three court cards: *malik* (king), *na'ib* (viceroy or deputy), and *thani na'ib* (second deputy or under-deputy).

Because of Muslim religious prohibitions against depicting living beings, designs were abstract rather than figured. The Persian suit of *jawkân* or polo sticks was unfamiliar to Europeans so they became *bastos* or cudgels in Spain and *bastoni* (meaning a ceremonial baton of office) in Italy.

The First Tarot Cards

No records survive to tell us exactly where, when, by whom, or why the first tarot cards were made. However, the oldest surviving cards (the *Cary-Yale Visconti* deck) were made for Filippo Visconti, the last Visconti duke of Milan. Probably painted as a wedding gift, this magnificent deck of overly large cards was hand-painted with hammered gold leaf illumination. Both the new game and the cards used to play it were originally called *trionfi* (triumphs or "trumps"), but by 1516 had become known as *tarocchi*—a name that is still used in Italy today. This word possibly refers to a technique called *taroccare* for stamping designs (*tara*) into sheets of gold, for it also refers to a Sicilian orange with a similarly golden, pitted surface. It may even be related to the Arabic word *taraqa*, which means "to hammer." However, this is only the latest in a long list of proposed meanings for *tarot* or *tarocchi* that range from the Egyptian "royal road" to the Buddhist goddess Tara to the Italian river Taro.

Woodcut tarot decks, of a more medieval design, appeared at some point during the century, with variations in design by region. The fifty-card *Tarocchi del Mantegna*, for instance, included cards such as the beggar, servant, artisan, and merchant, as well as many of the familiar Major Arcana cards, and culminated with the Prime Mover and First Cause. A deck known as the Charles VI or *Gringonneur Tarot* is actually a late-fifteenth century hand-painted deck of the northern Italian type (probably from Venice or Ferrara).

Renaissance Culture

Northern Italy in the early Renaissance had a culture made rich by the influx of Greek manuscripts and translators fleeing the crumbling Byzantine Empire. Anti-Semitic riots in Spain caused an early exodus to Italy of cultured and cosmopolitan Jews. Musicians came

from southern France, former home of the courtly love tradition, the heretic Cathars, and early writings of the Hebrew Qabala. Members of the nobility married throughout Europe, overseeing centers of international culture. The tarot may yet be heir to Pythagorean, Hermetic, Neo-Platonic, and magical thought as synthesized in Alexandria, Egypt. Filippo Maria Visconti, a great believer in scholarship and astrology, kept several learned philosophers on his staff. One of these was a Jewish astrologer named Helias (dare we assume he was also a Qabalist?), and another was Marziano da Tortona, who created an allegorical card game of Pagan gods in four suits. Painted images regularly served as memory devices but also as objects of spiritual contemplation and veneration. Allegorical games were popular. Some, based on various cosmological models, depicted a universe of meaning, showing a pattern and purpose to existence—a path for ascent and descent between the mortal earth and the seat of the divine godhead and eternal life. The second half of the tarot trumps bear an uncanny resemblance to common Renaissance images from the book of Revelation. In fact, a traveler in northern Italy today will find that tarot images are familiar themes among the Christian art from the fourteenth and fifteenth centuries. New York library researcher Gertrude Moakley saw the similarity between tarot images, Petrarch's poem *I Trionfi* (c. 1356), and pictures of triumphal festival parades. She also noted that card playing, in places where it was restricted by law, *was allowed* during the Saturnalia and Carnival festivities and was, in fact, rarely condemned by the church.

A Cosmological Game

Tarot may have arisen, therefore, out of allegorical games and art-of-memory teachings that were part of the standard emblem (allegorical symbol) tradition of the Renaissance. In such a cosmology, each stage triumphs over the previous ones in a kind of hierarchical order, leading from the lowliest figure up to God himself in the World card, depicted as a restored Jerusalem, Paradise, or Creation.

Using the order and titles of the trumps, recorded by a Dominican monk in *Sermones de Ludo Cum Aliis* ("Discourses on a Game (played) with Others" c.1450–1480), and following suggestions by Andrea Vitali and Gertrude Moakley, we can imagine a cosmological story that would be totally in keeping with fifteenth century ideas:

First comes the *bagatella* (Juggler) who is "lowest of all." (This person of "trifling importance" became the prototype for the *commedia dell'arte* figure known as *bagatino*, a mountebank spouting idiotic patter.) Next we encounter the worldly guides of *Imperatrix* (Empress) and *Imperator* (Emperor), followed by spiritual guidance that warns us against denying our Christian faith, *La papessa* (The Popess), and tells us to remain strong in sanctity, *El papa* (The Pope).

We are taught to moderate our lives, *La temperantia* (Temperance), to make us fit for "Love," *L'amore* (Love). Moreover, we must have victory over the mundane world, *Lo caro triumphale* (The Triumphal Cart), requiring resolution and strength, *La forteza* (Force). However, when we reach the height of our reign, fate turns the wheel, *La rotta* (The Wheel), and we descend the other side. Time and age bend us, *El gobbo* (The Hunchback), and as traitors, *Lo impichato* (The Hanged Man), we are powerless against death, *La morte* (Death). We proceed either to hell, *El diavolo* (The Devil), or through lightning and celestial fires, *La sagitta* (The Arrow), to the Heavenly Bodies above where we meet our fate: *La stella* (The Star), *La luna* (The Moon), *El sole* (The Sun). "And there shall be signs in the sun, and in the moon, and in the stars; and upon the earth distress of nations" Luke 21:25.

We will then be called before the Angel of the Last Judgment, *Lo angelo* (The Angel), where Divine Justice triumphs over all, *La iusticia* (Justice), and we enter into the presence of God, *El mondo, cioe Dio Padre* (The World, namely God the Father). Whether we fail to recognize God or do recognize him, we release all worldly attachments and become mad in the sight of the world. *El matto* (The Madman) is without any value (unless the players wish).

Divination With Cards

There is no clear record of divination with cards before the eighteenth century, however there are hints that tarot may have had such uses. A sixteenth-century poetry game called *tarocchi appropriate* features character analysis. Pietro Aretino, in *Le Carte Parlanti* (The Talking Cards, 1525), gives allegorical meanings to some of the tarot cards, stating, "They reveal the secrets of nature, the reason for things, and explain the causes why day is driven out by night and night by day." In 1540, Francesco Marcolino da Forli published a divination technique or *"sorti"* using playing cards as a randomizing device that directed the questioner to pages of his book containing predictions. However, the cards themselves did not have meanings. The Venetian courts of 1589 recorded evidence of the use of tarot cards on a Witch's altar and in a spell. Such use was explained by Pierre del'Ancre in 1622: "It is a type of divination of certain people who take the images and place them in the presence of certain demons or spirits that they have summoned, so that those images will instruct them on the things that they want to know." By 1665, John Lenthall in London was publishing a fifty-two–card fortunetelling deck. A sheet of thirty-five Bolognese trump and number cards from the early 1700s was labeled with simple divinatory meanings such as "journey," "betrayal," "married man," and "love." In 1765, Casanova wrote in his journal that his Russian peasant mistress read the cards every day, "laying them out in a square of twenty-five cards." Goethe, in his biography *Dichtung und Wahrheit*, tells how in the autumn of 1770, as the result of several playing-card readings, he experienced a painful situation regarding two sisters that was to influence all his later relationships with women. Also in 1770, Etteilla, in the first book ever on fortunetelling with playing cards, mentions *"les Taraux"* in a list of other methods of fortunetelling.

Birth of the Myths of the Divinatory Tarot

In 1781 the destiny of tarot took a major turn. Antoine Court de Gébelin announced in the eighth volume of his encyclopedia *Le Monde Primitif* that "there still exists in our time a work of the ancient Egyptians, one of their books which escaped from the flames that devoured their superb libraries and which contains the purist doctrine on interesting subjects." He included an essay on *The Book of Thot* by le Comte de M*** (Mellet) who explains for the first time that the cards correspond to letters of the Hebrew alphabet. De Mellet assigns *Aleph* to the World, and so on in descending order to the Fool as the last letter, *Tau*. Both de Gébelin and de Mellet were members of Masonic, Rosicrucian, and other secret societies that were rampant in France, so it is possible that they were revealing information that had already been circulating among these secret societies. This were the first source of the myths about the tarot that have come down to us today.

As a result of these myths, the sacred entered the tarot and lodged there as its soul. Myths define who we are and who we want to be. They are public lies, but they are unparalleled in illuminating inner, spiritual, and psychological truths. Dream analyst Jeremy Taylor writes that myths are "emotionally evocative, symbolically accurate, archetypal representations of what it feels like to encounter the deeper layers of the collective 'objective psyche.' . . . The stories give compelling symbolic narrative form to the deepest intuitions. Indeed, any story that succeeds in evoking that felt sense of participating in larger and more meaningful patterns of truth . . . is, by definition, a 'sacred narrative,' and will have a tendency to attract adherents who take it literally." Tarot scholar Robert O'Neill sums it up best: "De Gebelin's myth reawakened interest in this fundamental facet of the human experience. Thereafter, the tarot was not a game but a coherent symbolic system that provided insight into individual development. And the source of that concept was identified with Egyptian mystery and magic." This tarot myth seems to inform us that there is more to life than what we see and that initiation through myth opens us to other realms of experience which are believed to be documented in the tarot images. The tarot, for those who can understand the symbols, is a tool for accessing the forces that operate in those realms and influencing events through them.

De Mellet first called the suit of coins *talismants*. A. E. Waite used the term *pantacles* for Talismans and depicted Coins as Pentacles in his deck. He probably based his choice on what Eliphas Lévi wrote about the pentagram: that it is the "key to the two worlds . . . absolute philosophy and natural science" and is therefore the most perfect *pantacle*. De Gébelin called the cards *Atouts* (a word which means both trumps and chance or opportunity). He was first to use the terms High Priest and High Priestess, while de Mellet followed the designation of Jupiter and Juno used on Swiss-German decks like the *Swiss IJJ*. Cups represented the divining cup of Joseph; Coins or Talismans were the Theraphim, Urim, and Thummin; Swords divined the future and the fate of combats; and the Wands of Moses and the Magi worked their wonders. The Swords were royalty; Cups, the priesthood; Coins, commerce; and Batons (crosier or goad), agriculture. Finally, de Mellet describes how the Egyptian priests used what he called the *Tableaux* for the interpretation of dreams, giving as an example pharaoh's dream of seven fat cows and seven lean ones. Basically, he drew one or more cards for each image in the dream and then interpreted them.

Two years later, Jean-Baptiste Alliette, a print dealer and teacher of algebra (actually, numerology) who had produced several books on fortunetelling with playing cards under the pseudonym Etteilla, published his own meanings (including reversals) for the seventy-eight cards of the *Livre de Thot* (Book of Thoth). These meanings have influenced most subsequent divinatory meanings for the cards. He created his own tarot deck, radically changing the images and names of the cards.

Tarot and Magic

Eliphas Lévi (pseudonym for Alphonse-Louis Constant), who had been a deacon in the Catholic Church, picked up the esoteric trail in the 1850s with several works on magic. He related the number cards to the *sephiroth* of the Qabalistic Tree of Life and the suits to the elements. Then he proposed a system that differed from de Mellet's for relating the *Clefs* (Lévi's word for the Trumps, meaning "Keys") to the Hebrew letters, beginning with *Aleph* as the Magician.

Lévi's disciple Paul Christian (aka Jean-Baptiste Pitois) in *Histoire de la magie* (History of Magic, 1870) first used the term Arcana, "magical secrets," for the two groups of cards. The term, probably derived from the works of the Neo-Platonist Iamblichus, comes from *arca*, signifying a box or container, whose root means "to close or shut up." He described an Egyptian mystery school initiation under the Great Pyramid (based on a Neoplatonic work known

as the *Crata Repoa*) in which the initiate learned the secret meaning of the Sacred Arcana.

In the 1890s a group of learned French occultists gathered around Gerard Encausse, who wrote under the pseudonym of Papus, exploring and expanding on the magical ideas of Eliphas Lévi and the divinatory interpretations of Etteilla. He wrote *Tarot of the Bohemians* (1889), which also contains essays by several of his compatriots. One of these, Oswald Wirth, created the first published set of occult tarot cards based on the Qabala, which appear in Papus's book. In 1896 R. Falconnier published *Les XXII lames hermètiques du tarot divinatoire* (The 22 Hermetic Plates of the Divinatory Tarot) with all-new Egyptian-styled illustrations by M. O. Wegener based on the descriptions of Paul Christian. This began a tradition of esoteric Egyptian tarot decks that is still around today.

Meanwhile, in England, a magical organization called the Hermetic Order of the Golden Dawn was founded in 1888. Its rituals were based on a cipher manuscript that included an alternative to Eliphas Lévi's Qabalistic correspondences. The Golden Dawn is most renowned for its syncretic work on the doctrine of correspondences linking astrology, the Hebrew letters and Tree of Life, the tarot, plants, perfumes, angels, and magical weapons. Out of this tradition arose several decks and books written and created by Golden Dawn initiates: MacGregor and Moina Mathers (*The Golden Dawn Tarot*, c. 1890s), A. E. Waite and Pamela Colman Smith (*The Rider-Waite-Smith Tarot*, 1909), Aleister Crowley (*The Thoth Deck*, painted by Frieda Harris, 1944), and Paul Foster Case (*The BOTA Deck*, published 1947). The French continued a tradition of card reading influenced by Paul Marteau (owner of Grimaud publishing), whose 1948 book *Le Tarot de Marseille* revolutionized interpretations by closely examining subtle details of line and color in the cards.

The Modern Tarot Renaissance

In 1960, New York bookseller Eden Gray found a lack of easy-to-comprehend instructions for interpreting the tarot. As a result, she wrote and self-published the first of several books on the *Rider-Waite-Smith* deck that made it relatively easy for anyone to do a reading. She was the first person to use the term "Fool's Journey" and encouraged people simply to look at the images to determine their meanings. It was out of the alternative culture of the late 1960s and early 1970s, feeding into the "New Age," that the modern tarot Renaissance took root. By the end of the 1960s, artists were designing tarot cards that would express modern, mythic, metaphysical, pop- and cross-cultural themes. Since then hundreds of new books and decks have been published, as tarot evolved from a mere game or fortunetelling device to a tool and inspiration for meditation, self-growth, personal insight, and creativity.

The Buddha Tarot

Created and illustrated by Robert M. Place

Two of Double Vajras

- 79 full-color cards, black organdy pouch, and 72-page instruction booklet

- Cards are 2¾ x 4¾ with nonreversible backs and illustrated pips

- Spare line drawings and vivid colors evoke the traditional art of south Asia

The Descent from Tusita Heaven – The Fool

- Connects Eastern and Western spiritual experiences—from Buddhism to Pythagorean theory—and illustrates the parallels between the life of the Buddha and the Fool's Journey

- Explains the fundamentals of Buddhism as you follow the legend of Siddhartha on the path to enlightenment

Seven of Jewels

Aksobhya: The Buddha of Vajras

The Peacock: The Animal of Lotuses

Learning Tarot:
A Manageable Approach

by Elizabeth Genco

L et's face it: learning tarot can be a daunting prospect. The deck is big—seventy-eight cards big. In practice, the deck doubles in size if you consider reversed meanings. And once you've learned each card backward and forward (or right side up and upside down, even), you've got to apply that knowledge in readings, right? So just when is all of this learning supposed to happen?

If you're anything like I was way back when, the sheer magnitude of the task that is learning tarot may be keeping you from digging in. Personally, I avoided tarot for a solid decade because I thought that I'd have to spend years acquiring basic knowledge before the payoffs appeared. While it's true that tarot has a learning curve and you're not going to absorb it all overnight, you don't have to let that stop you from getting started. In fact, with the right approach and attitude, your practice can reap great rewards from the very beginning. Kick intimidation to the curb and keep the fun in your learning with these strategies.

1. Forget Reversed Meanings—For Now
Here's an idea that may surprise you: you don't have to read reversed cards if you don't want to. Yes, it's true that most readers interpret reversed cards and that reversals can add depth and clarity

to a reading. But there's no rule that says that you have to use them, especially when you're first starting out. In fact, one valid point of view states that the seventy-eight cards upright contain all the meanings necessary for a good reading.

Concentrate on learning those upright meanings first. That may sound obvious, but many a beginning practitioner (myself included) has been distracted by trying to get reversals "right" before learning the basics. Regardless of whether you read reversals, you'll still need to have a good handle on the upright meaning of the cards. And, since reversed meanings are often intimately tied to a card's upright meaning, getting that down pat will only strengthen your reversed interpretations, should you decide to use them later.

2. Study the Pip Cards First

Many authors place special emphasis on the Major Arcana, and rightly so—after all, those are the cards that tackle the philosophical and esoteric issues. But that doesn't mean that you have to learn them first. Similarly, the court cards can be some of the most difficult, confusing cards in the deck. Why struggle with all that up front when you're brand new to tarot? There's no shame in putting off the tougher stuff until a little bit later.

Instead of tackling the Majors from the get-go, consider spending time with the Ace through Ten cards (or "pips") of the Minor

Seven · Wands

The Seven of Wands from *The Victoria Regina Tarot*

Arcana first. These Minors deal with mundane, day-to-day issues. When tarot is completely new to you, those cards can be easier to understand and absorb because you relate to their issues already. One way to start is to learn the qualities associated with the various suits and some of the basic numerology associated with the numbers one through ten. Once you have those concepts down, apply them to the Aces through Tens of each suit. Cross reference your interpretations with those found in your favorite beginner book. By the time you're finished, not only will you have a grasp of

those cards and the suits, you'll be familiar with over half the deck.
Quite an accomplishment!

Whatever cards you choose to tackle first, throw yourself into
them head-on and don't worry so much about the others. You don't
have to learn every card at once. Eventually, they'll all get a turn.

3. Keep Your First Readings Small—Really Small

The little white booklet (or LWB) that comes with your first tarot
deck isn't going to tell you this, so I will: you don't have to start
reading with that old chestnut, the Celtic Cross spread. The Celtic
Cross is often passed off as a beginner's spread, but any spread
with ten cards is bound to be needlessly complicated for a beginner. That's not to say that the Celtic Cross isn't useful, just that
there may be better spreads to start with.

When you're starting to learn tarot, it can be daunting to try to
make sense of a complicated pattern of ten cards. Your first readings will be spent sitting there with your instruction book in one
hand and your notebook in the other. Making sense of what's in
front of you can be hard, so help yourself whenever possible.
Smaller spreads make it easy to cut your teeth on readings without
feeling overwhelmed. Try learning some simple spreads with just a
few cards, such as three-card spreads (mind-body-spirit, physical-
mental-emotional, etc.). There is no shortage of such layouts—lists
of them can be found on the Internet without much trouble, and
you can even make up your own (yes, you really can make up your
own spreads!). After you have spreads with a few cards down, try
spreads with four cards, then spreads with five, and so on.

There is nothing wrong with starting with spreads of two and
three cards, or even one. Master these, and you'll be performing
complicated readings before you know it.

4. Begin to Read Right Away

For many beginners, the idea of learning seventy-eight cards is
exhausting enough. But it's the idea of putting it all together in a
reading that really sends them over the edge. Will they "do it
right"? Will their readings be correct? Will they have one of those
grand mystical experiences rumored to follow bouts of prolonged
esoteric or spiritual practice? These concerns are beside the point
when you're just starting out. What's worse, they can suck all of
the enjoyment out of learning a new skill.

Instead of all that, try this: forget that you're a beginner, trust yourself, and start to read right away. Make reading less of an "event" and instead something that you do naturally by doing it all the time. Yes, you'll probably make mistakes. So what? Everyone makes mistakes. The process of reading becomes easier as you do it more often. Get used to applying your hard-earned knowledge from the very beginning, and in no time at all the act of reading will become instinctive. That instinct is exactly where your best readings will come from.

Another benefit of reading right away is that you'll get exposure to those cards that you don't yet know well. Even if you haven't studied certain cards, per se, there's no reason why you should avoid them. The more you see them, the more information you'll absorb about them, making them easier to learn when the time comes.

For your practice readings, you can read for friends, family, or anyone who will sit still long enough to get a reading. Also, despite rumors to the contrary, there is nothing wrong with reading for yourself. Indeed, why deny yourself personal guidance, which is one of the greatest benefits of learning tarot in the first place?

5. Lighten Up, or, There's No "One Right Way" to Do It

Ask a dozen tarot readers how to read tarot, and you'll get a dozen different answers. Take a look at the New Age section of any bookstore and you'll find scads of tarot books, each with a different approach to learning the deck. Speaking of decks, there are hundreds available, each with a different focus and point of view. So where does that leave you, the humble enthusiast just starting out on "the Fool's Journey"? Hopelessly confused, right?

Instead of confusion, let this abundance of ideas remind you that there's no one way to learn tarot but your way, and that your way is just as valid as anybody else's. Ultimately, your understanding of the cards will come from the mixture of the symbols on your deck, what you've learned from authors or teachers, and what your own intuition brings to the table. As such, no two people

will know the cards in exactly the same way. This frees you from the
pressure of having to conform to someone else's strict vision of what
the tarot is. Instead, you can create your own vision—and from
there create your own practice. That vision and practice is made one
card, spread, or reading at a time.

Breaking the task of learning the tarot down into smaller pieces
can make the difference between mastering the cards and giving up
in frustration. Allow your confidence to grow by taking on just a little bit at a time. Apply yourself with sincerity to the smaller tasks.
You may be amazed at what the tarot gives back.

Ship of Fools Tarot

Created and illustrated by Brian Williams

- 78 two-color cards and a 240-page illustrated book

- Cards are 2⅝ x 3¼, with reversible backs and illustrated pips

- The final tarot project of Brian Williams

- Extends the metaphor of the Fool's Journey through not only the Major Arcana but the entire deck

- Inspired by the much-loved classic of German culture, *Das Narrenschiff* (The Ship of Fools), by Sebastian Brant

- Merges classic *Rider-Waite-Smith* symbolism with *The Ship of Fools* iconography

O THE VAGABOND

SEVEN OF COINS

QUEEN OF STAVES

ACE OF CUPS

EIGHT OF SWORDS

A Meditation for the Majors

by Ruth Ann and Wald Amberstone

There are several ways you can approach learning the tarot. When it comes to a personal understanding of how to interpret the cards, an organic approach is usually best. Immerse yourself in the cards through contemplation, journey work, study, and practice. These methods will all lead you to unique insights that will support your tarot practice no matter how you choose to use the cards.

There are times, however, when good old-fashioned memorization is what's called for. One of the most fascinating aspects of learning the tarot, while simultaneously often the most challenging, is discovering and remembering the many correspondences that are associated with each card. Since there are so many correspondences to learn (key numbers, astrological attributions, esoteric functions and titles, etc.), it's tempting to ignore them entirely. You would be missing out on some very powerful tools in that case.

"How so?" you may ask. "Why, for instance, does it really matter whether or not I remember the key numbers of the Major Arcana? The pictures give me all the information I need to do a good reading." That may be true. But the key numbers and other correspondences can give you additional information so you can do a great reading!

We're going to teach you a simple exercise that works with any deck and is a powerful aid to help you remember the important correspondences for the cards of the Major Arcana. But first let's look at some of the reasons for knowing this information and how it can help you become a better reader.

Key Numbers

Even if you choose not to learn many of the esoteric correspondences that are available, we believe you should at least know the key numbers of the Major Arcana. Whatever deck you're using, the creator of that deck chose the order of the Majors for a reason. They tell the story of the deck. Ignoring that order is like trying to read a book when the chapters have been re-arranged.

In the *Rider-Waite-Smith* deck, the Major Arcana are numbered according to the chart below. Other decks may change the order slightly or have different names for the cards, so examine the deck you are working with for these variations. Also, many decks display the key number using roman numerals. You can use this exercise to learn those as well if you aren't already familiar with them.

When you're doing a reading, it's helpful to know which cards come before and after the ones that are on the table. If you know this, each card has the potential to be a Past-Present-Future spread of its own. (Yes, this can work with the Minor Arcana cards, too—but they're not as difficult to learn!) Of course, we're not recommending you read every card this way, but there will be times when it will be surprisingly appropriate.

Knowing the key numbers is essential if you're going to work with birth cards. Whether you use the Tarot School method or Mary Greer and Angeles Arrien's method, determining which Major Arcana cards are special to you or someone you know is based on a numerological reduction of your birthdate. In order to translate the results into cards, you'll need to know which numbers go with which cards.

Once you're comfortable with the key numbers, you'll find them most useful as a form of tarot shorthand. Use them to save time when you're taking notes or recording readings. You can also have fun "talking in code" with other tarot enthusiasts!

Astrological Attributions

Even if you're not an astrologer, knowing the astrological signs and planets associated with the Major Arcana can give you a great deal of additional information. For example, if the Devil appears in a spread, the beginning of winter (Capricorn) may be an important time to consider in the context of the reading. The more you know about the qualities of the signs and planets associated with the cards, the more useful information you'll have available to work with. However, the first step is learning which sign or planet goes with which card.

The table below includes a list of widely accepted astrological correspondences. (You may find other systems of attribution elsewhere.)

There are also astrological attributions for the entire Minor Arcana. You can easily find that information with a little research if you're interested in learning those as well.

#	Roman Numeral	Card Name	Astrological Attribution
0	0	The Fool	Uranus
1	I	The Magician	Mercury
2	II	The High Priestess	Moon
3	III	The Empress	Venus
4	IV	The Emperor	Aries
5	V	The Hierophant	Taurus
6	VI	The Lovers	Gemini
7	VII	The Chariot	Cancer
8	VIII	Strength	Leo
9	IX	The Hermit	Virgo
10	X	Wheel of Fortune	Jupiter
11	XI	Justice	Libra
12	XII	The Hanged Man	Neptune
13	XIII	Death	Scorpio
14	XIV	Temperance	Sagittarius
15	XV	The Devil	Capricorn
16	XVI	The Tower	Mars
17	XVII	The Star	Aquarius
18	XVIII	The Moon	Pisces
19	XIX	The Sun	Sun
20	XX	Judgment	Pluto
21	XXI	The World	Saturn

Esoteric Functions

One of the most interesting, fun, and potentially useful sets of correspondences is the esoteric functions. These are magical attributions that were assigned to the Major Arcana by the Order of the Golden Dawn. We have found them to be surprisingly helpful in revealing important hidden interpretations that you won't find by looking at the pictures.

You can use the cards with double functions to help with reading reversals. An upright card would indicate the first of the functions mentioned and a reversal would indicate the second function. Even the cards that have only one function have two clearly different versions of that function. For example, the Emperor has the function of sight. Reversed, it could mean blindness or the inability to "see." Justice has the function of work. Reversed, it could mean not working or that something has malfunctioned.

Card	Esoteric Function
The Fool	Element of Air
The Magician	Life & Death
The High Priestess	Peace & War
The Empress	Wisdom & Folly
The Emperor	Sight
The Hierophant	Hearing
The Lovers	Smell
The Chariot	Speech
Strength	Taste
The Hermit	Sexuality (Touch)
Wheel of Fortune	Riches & Poverty
Justice	Work
The Hanged Man	Element of Water
Death	Movement
Temperance	Anger
The Devil	Laughter
The Tower	Indignation & Grace
The Star	Imagination
The Moon	Sleep
The Sun	Fertility & Barrenness
Judgment	Element of Fire
The World	Power & Servitude

The Order of Majors Meditation

The meditation we are about to show you will help you to easily learn and absorb these important correspondences. It can also be used to help you remember other connections such as esoteric titles, keywords, intelligences, etc. The sample exercise will focus on the key numbers, but the technique remains the same for any group of associations you wish to learn. And although the emphasis here is on the cards of the Major Arcana, this meditation can be used with the Minors as well.

Preparation

Before beginning any practice of tarot, you may want to wash your hands and face in cool water. This is a little bit of magical practice that will help prepare your body to anchor and contain an enhanced state.

Pick a quiet time and place to work. Prepare your space and set out your materials: your deck, the list of correspondences you want to commit to memory, plus any ritual implements you might want present. Establish quiet in your surroundings and inside yourself.

Take a moment to express your intent, either silently or out loud, to give your undivided attention to what you are about to do.

To bring yourself quickly and easily into a meditative state, you can use a simple technique we call "Breathe and Relax."

Close your eyes. Breathe naturally. Pay attention to your breath and notice if you restrain it in any way. Relax your chest and throat and let your belly become soft and round. Let thoughts come and go as they will. Check the rest of your body for any muscular contraction and let it go. Allow yourself to relax your body and your breath as much as you can in the space of a few minutes. When you are ready, open your eyes but remain in a meditative state.

Throughout the remainder of your meditation/study session, mental focus should come easily while you continue to breathe naturally and stay relaxed. This alternation of relaxation and attention is a practice that is very well rewarded. If you can develop the patience, it will pay rich dividends to do this miniature meditation before each separate part of any learning process, clearing the mind the way a wine taster clears his palate between each sip of every vintage.

The Meditation

Extract from your deck all the cards of the Major Arcana. Place the Fool faceup in front of you. On the Fool place the Magician, faceup. Then put the High Priestess on top of the Magician, and then place the rest of the Major Arcana faceup in ascending rank order, creating an ordered stack. When you are done, the World will be faceup on top of the stack in front of you. Then turn the entire stack facedown so that the World is on the bottom of the stack.

Breathe and relax. When your breath is regular, your body relaxed, and your mind calm, you are ready to begin.

Take a deep breath and at the bottom of the exhalation, turn over the top card. This will be the Fool. On your next breath, as you breathe in, mentally say the number of the key, which is "Zero." As you breathe out, say the name of the key, which is "The Fool." "Zero" on the in-breath. "The Fool" on the out-breath.

At the bottom of the out-breath, without breaking the rhythm of your breathing, turn over the next card. This will be the Magician. Place it squarely and neatly on top of the Fool. As you breathe in, mentally say the number "One." As you breathe out, say the name "The Magician." "One" on the in-breath. "The Magician" on the out-breath.

At the bottom of the out-breath turn the next card, place it neatly over the Magician (neatness is important here), and repeat the process of mentally saying the number of the card on the in-breath and its name on the out-breath.

Repeat this process with all the cards in the stack of Majors, ending with the World.

Be sure to use only one breath per card, no more. This is important because the learning process depends on the steady rhythm of the breath.

Now reverse the process.

Once again, as you breathe in, say "Twenty-one." And as you breathe out, say the name "The World." "Twenty-one" on the in-breath. "The World" on the out-breath.

Then turn the World card facedown to begin a new, facedown stack. The card that is now revealed on the faceup stack will be 20—Judgment.

On the next in-breath, mentally continue with the number "Twenty." On the out-breath, mentally continue with the word "Judgment." At the end of the exhalation, turn 20—Judgment facedown and continue the exercise with 19—The Sun, etc., until you reach the end of the faceup stack with O—The Fool. When you have turned the Fool facedown, the meditation is complete.

Do this exercise as an open-eyed meditation, with a measured and regular breathing pattern and complete concentration. Perform this meditation once a day until you can call up the correspondences at will. Even advanced students will experience considerable benefit from this practice, and for beginners it is essential. Remember to go slowly, taking the time to absorb what you learn from this practice.

Advanced Work

You can continue to work with this meditation even after you have mastered whichever correspondences you have chosen to learn. This advanced work is done without looking at the cards.

Use the "Breathe and Relax" technique to bring yourself into a meditative state. Then, with your eyes closed, bring the image of each card in order before your mind's eye, if you can, or simply name it if you can't visualize it. Mentally say its number (or other correspondence) on the in-breath, and clear the image from your mind as you finish the out-breath.

When you have finished the entire cycle of Majors both forward and backward, take three deep breaths and open your eyes.

Those Darned Court Cards

by Thalassa

After the eager tarot student has begun to grasp the larger-than-life concepts and mastered the workaday minutiae of the tarot, there remains one more component to study, filled with potential, but rife with enigma. Between the drama of the Majors and the mundane panoply of the Minors, there is a speed bump on the road to grasping the entire tarot deck as a coherent and energized whole. In books and classes, the court cards are often neglected stepchildren, dismissed with a pat on the head before heading off to more dramatic business.

The Major Arcana encompasses the "big ticket items"—the archetypes that underpin human experience, the profound crises and epiphanies that represent landmarks in life. The majestic procession of the Majors taps into the wellspring of myth and the labyrinth of the human saga. Certainly, the Major Arcana gets a lot of attention—many books hardly even touch upon anything else. It is the eight hundred-pound gorilla of the tarot: dramatic, mysterious, and hard to ignore.

The numbered cards of the Minor Arcana represent the "nuts and bolts" of everyday existence. The range of the ordinary—the cycles and processes of life—is covered through pip cards of each suit. The nature of existence is such that even while one is going through a crisis or a life transition, one still (we assume) has to get out of bed and go to work each day, addressing mundane concerns like taking out the garbage and paying bills. The Minors illustrate how life continues with its commitments and requirements even as we experience the nurturing inspiration of the Empress or the grueling education of the Tower.

And then there are those darned court cards.

The earliest tarot and playing card decks included between three and six "people" cards for use in games, and when the tarot deck began to acquire occult and divinatory functions, the court cards—by now reduced to four per suit—became a sort of Cinderella component of the deck, used for representing people in spreads but not particularly noticed otherwise. The time has come to address this neglect and to accord the ladies and gents of the pasteboard parade their due.

Much writing on the court cards is pretty discouraging if one is looking for depth or heft in interpretation, and this seems a waste of sixteen perfectly good cards. For example, a typical definition of the Queen of Swords: "a dark woman who has suffered much." How dark? How much suffering—a constant buffeting by fate or a lifetime of bad haircuts? How about the Knight of Wands: "an impetuous, fair-haired young man." Aren't most of us impetuous when we're young? Is he naturally fair or is it peroxide? Are we only the sum of our hair and eye color, like some substandard astral dating service? What if the person working with the cards, or being read for, is not of European descent and is therefore not in the sug-

gested pigment range? Instead of a mere supporting cast of characters to the action and adventure of the tarot, there are more rich
and varied possibilities of interpretation and use.

The Golden Dawn, and especially Crowley, created a system
wherein the elements of air, earth, fire, and water manifested themselves within the structure of the traditional court. Knights (which
correspond to Kings in many decks) are associated with the element of fire, Queens with water, Princes (Knights in many decks, for
extra confusion points) with air, and Princesses (Pages) with earth.
Those uncomfortable with the medieval hierarchy of King, Queen,
Knight, Page have reinterpreted the court to accommodate different
structures of relationships and elemental power. Among the
numerous examples such as the Man/Woman/Child/Sage court of
Jim Wanless's *Voyager* deck, the Father/Mother/Son/Daughter of
Joseph Martin's *Quest Tarot*, and Child/Seeker/Guardian/Guide in
Isha Lerner's *Inner Child Cards*, one sees the components renegoti-
ated in different ways. Other decks give a tribal spin or ethnic twist,
but whether in the sweeping velvet robes of the Renaissance, gothic
leather and lace, or beads and furs of a more rough-hewn time, the
archetypes retain their resonant importance.

One of the most challenging aspects of working with court cards
is integrating them into readings, where they represent the work-
ings and manifestations of human interaction. They can reveal
aspects of the self and—just as important—the reactions and interactions of people in the subject's life. Challenges and sources of
support can be identified and explored as they appear in readings.
By looking at the cards as reflections of personality and behavior,
this approach affords an opportunity to construct more nuanced
and personalized interpretations.

We can look at the courts as the constellation of experience,
illustrations of the matrices—individual and collective—that we
form within ourselves and with each other in relationships. Our
reactions to others are often tempered by the topography of our
inner landscapes, and we act as both mirrors and lenses to one
another; we can often see faults or strengths more clearly in
another than in ourselves. Relationships—good or bad, fleeting or
lasting, superficial or deep—are the result of the intersecting points
of our inner and outer selves with those of the people around us.
The court cards can be used as interpretive devices to help identify
and work with these facets of relationship with self and others.

Each court card can be viewed as a different facet of expression as they appear in the elements of each suit. They can be used to examine parts of the self and others to gain information and insight. Pages can represent the new or untried, youth (at any age), and a lack of experience (but the presence of potential). Knights can indicate the drive to movement, activity, competition, and challenge. Queens may represent nurturing and supportive roles, but also the ability to place limits and make alterations when necessary. Kings can be associated with achievement and authority (and our attitudes towards authority will often color our reactions to it in a tarot encounter), but can also carry a sense of—or need for—accountability. We can see and work with these energies constantly within ourselves, a confident expert (King of Swords) in one area of life, an anxious amateur in another (Page of Cups).

One can use the individual cards to create dialogue and interaction, constructing dioramas of existing or projected experience. One could even set up a "Court Card Theatre" for them to strut and fret their interactions and expressions in a decorative fashion as one contemplates their meanings and potentials.

Another way to view court cards is as a map of the path, or paths, by which energy and inspiration flow. Ideas can come from an informed consciousness or grow from previously unknown or untapped inner depths. Energy can move as the lightning bolt that flashes from the top of the Tree of Life to the bottom (Kether to Malkuth for the Qabalistically inclined), i.e. an idea forms from a wealth of experience and then works its way to manifestation. An individual trained and accomplished in a discipline may conceive an idea and work it to fruition, using his or her experience and knowl-

edge to overcome obstacles and make the necessary adjustments. Conversely, like the serpent that coils up the Tree of Knowledge, energy moves from unschooled darkness and into the light of accomplishment. Inspiration in the hands of someone as yet untrained can work though a different set of processes that includes learning and growth as part of the achievement of a goal.

Looking at the court cards this way, the Pages can be seen as a reflection of potential—the new or untested within us, the "beginner's mind." Knights can be seen as movement and passion, the drive to achieve that pushes a project or idea through difficulties or doldrums. Queens can be viewed as the evaluation process, the crucible of refinement, the period of final gestation. Kings may be seen as authority, the mastery of an endeavor, a pinnacle of experience, accomplishment, and visible results and rewards. The Page of Cups can therefore illustrate the spirit of openness and newness in the realm

Queen ◦ Swords

of emotion, intuition, the inner and spiritual realms, whereas as the Page of Swords might imply accessibility to new ideas and mental agility, an ability to think differently about an issue. The Knight of Wands can represent the drive to succeed, the push to maintain confidence and energy in the face of obstacles, but the Knight of Pentacles might indicate a need for slow and steady progress, for more careful work to guide an action forward to realization. The Queen of Cups can indicate a need to indulge in fantasy, fluid creativity, or spiritual inspiration to refine and clarify an endeavor, but the Queen of Swords can indicate that logical action and insightful thinking might be more effective to smooth rough edges and get a project completed with clarity and grace. The King of Swords can show how the mastery of mental disciplines, an ability to think clearly and act decisively, can achieve desired ends, whereas the King of Pentacles may indicate that a careful, pragmatic strategy gets one to the finish line.

The court cards can also function as assistants to magical and meditation processes. To rekindle wonder and loosen up one's mental and emotional muscles, consult a Page. To energize and focus, enlist the aid of a Knight for purpose, direction, and drive. To find nurturance and refining guidance, call upon a Queen. To engender confidence and remind yourself of your power, put a King in your corner.

The Queen of Swords from *The Victoria Regina Tarot*

39

By expanding the interpretation and utility of the courts in these varying directions we can amplify their interpretive and overall usefulness. The art is to discover what each court card is saying to you—and it is probably saying more than you initially thought.

This article contains material from Thalassa's forthcoming book on tarot.

Your Daily Inspiration

by Elizabeth Genco

The practice of picking a card every day is a standard tool in any beginning tarotist's arsenal—and a well-worn one in that of an old hand. Countless teachers and books recommend the practice to beginners, and it's an easy way for seasoned practitioners to stay on top of their game.

But what, exactly, do you do with that card? Sure, you dutifully write down the meanings in your tarot journal (you are keeping a journal, aren't you?), but you may have asked yourself if there's anything more to it than that.

In fact, there is. With a little creativity, the rudimentary card-a-day practice becomes a fun and unique way to learn tarot. Here are a few ideas for getting the most out of your card-a-day.

Close Observation

"Close Observation" is a technique taught by Wald and Ruth Ann Amberstone, founders of the Tarot School in New York City. Sometimes, when you're just learning how to read tarot, you may get so caught up in "what the cards mean" that you miss some important details—namely, the symbols that give the cards their meaning in the first place. "Close Observation" is a way of becoming intimately familiar with those symbols.

Spend a few minutes (three or four) looking closely at your chosen card. Make a mental inventory of every detail that you can. Take notice of people, locales, colors, objects, names, and numbers. While you're doing this, take care not to make any interpretations. Your job is simply to observe and absorb.

After you've studied the card for a few minutes, put it away and make a list of every detail that you can remember, no matter how small or insignificant it may seem. When you're sure you can't remember anything more, take a look at the card and see what you've missed. You may be surprised, even if you've been working with the tarot for a while.

As you become familiar with the pictures on the cards, you'll discover whole other interpretations that may go beyond the old standards. You'll be able to draw on the symbolism that's right in front of you when you're stuck in readings. Of course, the more well-versed you are in the symbolism of the cards, the more rich and meaningful those readings will be.

More information on the practice of "Close Observation" can be found in the Amberstones' book, *Tarot Tips*.

One-Card Reading

Not surprisingly, the card-a-day practice works well for one-card readings. You can use your daily card to answer a particular question you have that day, or just to see what's in store for the next twenty-four hours. Some readers use their card-a-day practice to address specific issues in their lives, such as finding a new job or getting out of debt. You can do this by ruminating on that issue

before selecting your card, then interpreting that card in terms of the message it has for you with regard to that specific issue for that day.

If you use your daily card to perform a one-card reading, be sure to firmly state your intention—in your mind or on paper—before selecting your card. Before you go to bed, think about your initial interpretation in light of what happened that day. Did events come to pass as you envisioned them? Was a different interpretation of the card more applicable in the end? Record your interpretations and the day's events in your journal.

Tarot Hide-and-Seek

One of my favorite card-a-day practices is a simple yet extremely useful game that I like to call "Tarot Hide-and-Seek." Select your card at the beginning of the day or the night before. Ask yourself, "Where will this card show up throughout my day?" Ask the universe to show you that card in the day ahead. Then watch like a hawk for the card to appear.

Part of the fun (and a great deal of the learning) in this practice is that the cards will show themselves in both obvious and unexpected ways. For example, the Queen of Pentacles might be that woman you spy feeding her children lunch in a park, or the Lovers may be lounging under a tree nearby. You may have a run-in with the Emperor during a business meeting, or maybe you get a glimpse of the Wheel of Fortune in a phone call from out of the blue.

Keep your mind open and your curiosity healthy. If you don't stumble across the meaning of the card during the day (you may not, and that's okay) that doesn't mean that the card failed to manifest. Maybe you saw a stuffed lion in a toy store on a day that you picked the Strength card. Maybe you came across roses or lilies (or better yet, both) in a garden on a day that you picked the Magician. The symbols of the tarot can be found all around us; they become more familiar and more real if you keep your eyes open for them. And you may be amazed at where and when they turn up.

This exercise is a great way to familiarize yourself with the many different meanings of the cards. Every tarot card, whether from the Minor or Major Arcana, is loaded with symbolism and layers of meaning. The meanings of the cards aren't going to be the same in every instance. The world around you is bound to show you some deep and unexpected aspects of the cards. The idea here is to be receptive to the possibilities.

Over time, the tarot will become less of a system of random meanings and more of a symbolic language. The better you learn that language, the more useful the tarot will be for you.

Write It Out

If you enjoy the freedom that comes from being creative, or if you just want to add a goofy, fun element to the lengthy and sometimes

XI FORTITUDE

Strength from *Medieval Enchantment: The Nigel Jackson Tarot*

cerebral exercise of learning the deck, try using your daily cards for literary inspiration. After you've selected your card and thought about its meaning for a few minutes, sit down with a notebook (perhaps your tarot journal) and a pen. Take some notes. Jot down some random thoughts. Set a timer and write about the card, not lifting your pen from the paper for the allotted time (try ten or fifteen minutes), letting the words flow as they may, no matter how off-the-wall they may seem. Study the picture on the card and make up a story about what you see. Or make up a story involving the meaning of the card.

Tarot cards express an unlimited amount of ideas, any number of which can be the basis for a piece of writing. Writing things down can crystallize meanings or help you work through difficult concepts. Your subconscious may produce an interpretation in writing that you never would have thought of otherwise. Show up at the page with an open mind and see what you can learn from yourself.

Explore Different Decks

If you're like most tarot people, it won't be long before the siren call of literally hundreds of decks will beckon to you from bookstores, gift shops, and online auctions. Most tarot readers are also collectors; you may find yourself sharing space with new additions to your "tarot family" whether you counted on it or not. If you're like a lot of folks, you'll maybe have a deck or two to read with, a few to meditate with, and several others that are just . . . sitting there. A daily card practice is a perfect way to play around with those all-too-often unused decks.

When using a different deck for your card-a-day, study the symbols on the cards you pick, admire the artwork, or read the creator's book provided with the deck. You'll add to your understanding of the cards by seeing things from another viewpoint. You can pick cards from a certain deck for a couple of days or work your way through an entire deck over several months. You'll get exposure to another creator's take on tarot without having to make the commitment that learning an entire deck entails. You may come to realize that you don't like a certain deck as much as you thought you did, which can be useful information in its own right.

Another idea for working with other decks is to pull a specific card from a few different decks. You'll get a feeling for the rich variations in how the same issues in the cards can be expressed in different ways.

Carry It Around

Sometimes, when you're just learning about a new card, it helps to make reference to it several times a day. You can do this by carrying the card with you.

This practice becomes even more helpful if you make use of the card in some mundane fashion. If you live in a city and take public transportation, you may find yourself reading on a train or a bus. Why not use the card as a bookmark for the day and take a few extra seconds to gaze at it as you make your way through the pages of your current novel? Your subconscious will work out the issues of that card in the background of your mind. Several decks come in smaller sizes, with cards that would easily fit into a wallet or checkbook. Or you can keep your card in your appointment book.

Purchasing a separate deck for this practice is probably a good idea, since there is a possibility that you'll lose a card or two.

If choosing a card every day seems like drudgery, make it work *for* you with one of these ideas or one of your own. Before long, you'll watch your knowledge and enjoyment of tarot bloom like flowers after a rainstorm.

A Closer Look At:

Golden Dawn Magical Tarot

Created and illustrated by
Chic and Sandra Tabatha Cicero

- 79 full-color cards and a 192-page mini-book in a slipcase

- Cards are 4⅝ x 3¼, with nonreversible backs and plain pips

- Merges the teachings of the Hermetic Order of the Golden Dawn with the symbolism of tarot

- Each card shows the proper Hebrew letters, planetary icons, and zodiacal symbols needed for use in Golden Dawn rituals

- Clearly illustrates and explains the connections between the Qabala and the tarot

A New View: Reversals

by Mary K. Greer

How do I read reversed cards—the ones that appear upside down in a spread?" "Why bother with reversals at all?" The fact is that you don't have to use reversed cards—many tarot readers don't. Nevertheless, they can add significant depth, tone, and subordinate ideas to the upright meaning of a card. They were first used in 1770 by Etteilla (aka Jean-Baptiste Alliette), whose book on fortunetelling with playing cards used a piquet deck with only thirty-two cards. To increase the number of portents Etteilla added reversed meanings. When he published divinatory meanings for the tarot in 1783, they included this recently invented technique that featured both opposing meanings and odd concepts that had no precedent in terms of the upright meanings.

Essentially, reversals encourage us to see things from a different and more complex point of view. It is the reader's decision whether or not to use them, as is the choice of what they are to signify.

Receiving too many reversals can make you feel like you have been dealt a "losing hand," but that's not necessarily so. Despite their rich potential, reversals are sadly read in overly limited or simplistic ways. If you wish, you can characterize each card as good or bad or use any other duality. Still, it's a fallacy that a reversal always switches the positive and negative attributes of the card—even though it may sometimes do so. When seen primarily as negative, reversals needlessly emphasize the irrational fears and suspicions that gather around the creative gifts of the spirit and psyche.

Since everything in a reading has significance, I have come to appreciate that a card appearing upside down adds special nuances and, sometimes, their own unique messages. In my readings I emphasize clarifying goals and the conscious creation of what you want in your life. Problematic cards represent energy that may be constrained and can be liberated. While reversals are not evil, they do, sometimes, represent adversity—but it's the kind that teaches us what we are capable of, that teaches us what really counts and what is truly important, that tests our moral fiber and character. By struggling with reversals we learn to respond with integrity and a determination not to turn away from the teachings of each circumstance.

Since none of the cards are absolutely good or bad, we have to look at all their meanings from the most problematic to the most helpful. The Sun, for instance, can be happiness and joy or sunburn. It can bring enlightenment or burnout. Traditionally, when reversed, the Sun's effects are weakened rather than eliminated. We might assume that the experience of either joy or burnout might be denied or resisted. From another perspective, the reversal can tell you to look for the inner Sun and its spiritual guiding light rather than seeing it only as an external source.

One reason why reversals are so difficult is that they take us to a place where we are most uncomfortable: the realm of the soul. Many of us know or reach this place only through dis-ease, that is, what takes us out-of-ease. For instance, traditional and modern interpretations for reversed cards often indicate stress-producing situations that could eventually manifest as illness. Remember, though, that stress builds muscle. Reversals also show us the positive motivations behind stress. In fact, the reversal often contains its own antidote.

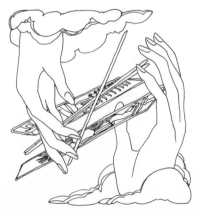

Using Reversed Cards

Any spread can be used with reversed cards. A reading consists of three elements: (1) the meaning of the card, combined with (2) the spread position's designated meaning, in terms of (3) the question asked. For instance, one of the most basic spreads has three positions: past, present, and future. The positions require you to switch tense from past to present to future as you interpret each card in response to the question.

To obtain reversals, shuffle or mix the cards facedown, in any way you prefer, so that the top of some cards are turned toward the bottom—head to foot. Lay out the cards in your usual spread. Most people turn the cards over from right to left, like turning the page of a book. The important thing is to find a technique that works for you and then be consistent. If you thoroughly mix the deck, it is "normal" to have half your cards reversed. It is still within the norm to have six or even seven out of ten cards reversed.

In general, it helps to think of reversed cards as "red flags," indicating that you should pay extra attention to them. They signal that something is not operating as usual. Upright cards tend to be conscious, outer, automatic, in process, and available. Reversed cards often indicate choice points, where you must be attentive. They may require conscientious, willful handling if you are to take full advantage of the energies and opportunities. It is like knowing that a car has a tendency to pull to the right and that you have to keep alert and make adjustments for it; or, they are places to stop struggling, relax, and let go of all expectations.

Some readers will not read a spread with too many reversals, but consider how awful a querent would feel as the result of such a refusal. Instead, see if there is an overall theme, like delay or denial, and then read the cards upright but with this slant. The few cards that were originally upright will likely show the greatest areas of support and leverage. Being more obvious and automatic, they can provide an opening or impetus to action. Rule number one is, *know the basic meanings for each card ranging from its most beneficial to most problematic possibilities.*

Interpreting Reversals

There are many ways to read a reversal. The following list includes the major techniques that show how a reversal can modify the card's upright meaning(s). Although some people find that they use only one to three of these, try all the possibilities until you find which methods work best for you. Eventually you'll want to pick methods that are most in alignment with your personal reading style and worldview. More information on these techniques can be found in *The Complete Book of Tarot Reversals* (Llewellyn, 2002).

1) *Blocked or resisted*
The energy normally described by the card may be blocked, repressed, denied, rejected, or resisted.

2) *Projected*
There could be a tendency to project denied material onto others. These may be qualities you admire as well as those you do not like.

3) *Delayed, difficult, unavailable*
There could be hesitation, uncertainty, unavailability, or an external delay. With many cards reversed, overall change may take longer than expected. Energy flows less smoothly or automatically than it would otherwise.

4) *Inner, unconscious, private*
The energy might be unconscious, inner, or private rather than conscious, outer, or public. Remember too that if the energy is truly unconscious the querent may not recognize it.

5) *New or Dark Moon (and other Round Deck variations)*
This suggestion is based on the round decks such as the *Motherpeace Tarot*. The reversal signifies the Dark or New Moon phase: unconscious, instinctual, hidden. It is the moment of interior conception and reformation.

6) *Breaking through, overturning, refusing, changing direction*
The querent could be overturning, getting out from under, breaking free of, rejecting, refusing, or turning away from the condition pictured. It can also show the end or passing away of a situation, a loosening, or a change in direction.

7) *No, or not [the upright meaning]; lacking*
Occasionally you can preface a standard upright interpretation with "no" or "not." Or try adding prefixes such as "non-" or "un-" to upright meanings. Take care that this does not lead to a judgmental, overly deterministic, or negative attitude.

8) *Excessive, over- or undercompensating*
The reversal may intensify or lessen the meaning of the card, or take it to extremes and overindulgence: too little or too much, under- or overdeveloped, immature or senile. In psychological terms it can indicate over- or undercompensation, or a tendency to flip dramatically between polarities.

9) *Misused or misdirected*
Misfiring, misuse, or misdirection implies a faulty start, bad timing, or something that is not used appropriately.

10) *"Re-" words: retried, retracted, reviewed, reconsidered*
Reversals immediately suggest other "re-" words such as those above. The prefix "re-" denotes backwards motion, withdrawal, opposition, negation, or to do again. We review, reconsider, and redo previous actions.

11) *Rectification: disease into remedy*
Reversals can be considered as both the disease (or at least the stress that may lead to disease) and the remedy: "What won't kill you will heal you." Sometimes, by going deeply into the reversal, seeking the causes and not just the effects, and experiencing all the excesses, we can break through to the other side.

12) *Unconventional, shamanic, magical, humorous*
If an upright card depicts conventional wisdom, then the reversal illustrates unconventional wisdom. It questions all the assumptions and suggests viewing things from a different perspective.

Additionally, a reversed card sometimes carries similar meanings to the upright meaning of the *preceding* card in the deck. The new energy cannot fully manifest due to past attachments of the previous card. Perhaps you need to go back and revisit its lessons or experiences. Thus, a reversal can "throw you back" or "revert you" to the naturally preceding card (thanks to Rita Moore and Sherryl Smith). The Five of Wands reversed might reflect back on

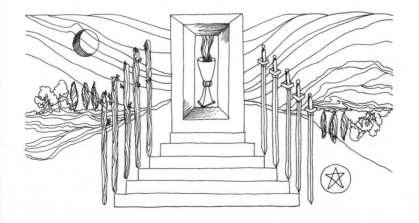

the Four of Wands, or the Star reversed asks you to consider the lessons of the Tower. Aces could revert to Tens. The innocent Fool harks back to the ignorant Fool, and Pages revert to dependent children in the Tens of their suit.

In actual practice, several characteristics may be at work with a single reversed card. The italicized words in the following example demonstrate the "twelve ways" using words related to each concept but not necessarily mentioned above. See if you can recognize which of the twelve ways most pertains to each possibility mentioned.

The Empress reversed—whose upright meanings include being feminine, nurturing, and relating—can indicate *not* acting in a feminine way. If we look deeper, this may be because you are *breaking through* family patterns of nurturing, or *resisting* the influence of your mother who is *emotionally unavailable* to you. You might, however, see your actions as *empowering* rather than *lacking*, especially if you are *inwardly questioning* society's expectations of women in order to discover how to be feminine *without* having to fulfill everyone else's needs and expectations. So you could be *countering* the norm, and exploring the full *range* of the *divine feminine*.

Look to other cards in the spread for repetitions of a theme, symbol, color, or action that support a particular nuance. For instance, the Ten of Swords reversed with the Ace of Wands (Ten becomes an Ace and the bright color takes over completely) could indicate that you have broken through an old cycle (are no longer pinned down), to a new beginning. The Star reversed with the Three of Cups might signify group libations rather than private ones (both have cups). Alternatively, the Star reversed accompanying the Six of Wands

reversed could indicate that your self-esteem falters when your accomplishments go unnoticed by others (private self-esteem becomes public pride, riding for a fall).

Sometimes the reversed card suggests a new image or picture. For instance, one person saw the parallel swords in the Nine of Swords reversed as a ladder into the cellar. The window in the Five of Pentacles reversed becomes a door. The swords in the Three and Ten of Swords reversed seem to fall out of both the heart and the person's back.

My favorite method is to ask the querent to literally describe the upright card (no interpretation allowed at this stage) including the attitudes, feelings, or mood of the figure(s) in it. Using what you know about the upright meaning, listen for anomalies, that is, any deviations or departures from the norm. For instance, if the querent describes the person in the upright Nine of Pentacles (traditionally a card of financial gain) as unhappy and anxious, then you know what the reversal is. Check to see if obvious money or property problems are causing the unhappiness. If not, then look for where there is a lack of inner security.

Don't be afraid to review several possible interpretations with the querent and ask which fits best. For instance, more than one person has felt that a reversed King expressed his mother's personality better than his father's.

In summary, reversed cards often express the extremes that exist naturally in a card's entire range of meaning. Always consider the whole realm of possibility, look for confirmation in other cards, get feedback from the querent, and consider whether several methods could be simultaneously correct, thus adding depth to your reading.

Keywords for Reversals

Aces: Delays, opportunities not grasped, impotency, inner focus.

Twos: Disharmony, opposition, duplicity, breaking the stalemate.

Threes: Nonworking, inaction, recovery, forging inner agreement.

Fours: Insecurity, rashness, loss of control, premonitions, divesting of restrictions, a strong inner foundation.

Fives: Inertia, dogma, repression, victimization, conformity, hope, renewed interest, reconciliation, gratification.

Sixes: Vanity, estrangement, self-actualization, insubordination.

Sevens: Arrogance, deceit, paranoia, embarrassment, cowardice, focus, design, constancy, implementation.

Eights: Lack of persistence, poor judgment, precipitous action, spiritual progress, generosity, expansiveness.

Nines: Lacking discipline and self-awareness, dependency, hostility, inner wisdom, humane compassion, nonphysical gain.

Tens: Rebellion, losses, quarrels, short-lived results, release.

Pages: Immature, gullible, depressed, closed down, ignorant, vulnerable, poor start, bad news, inner child, undeveloped potential.

Knights: Fanatical agents of elemental forces, reckless or reined-in impulses, destructive, irresponsible, inner quests.

Queens: Selfish, unwise use of power and control, inconstant, weak, absent, unfeminine, nagging or smothering, overthrowing parental or societal strictures and authority, the inner feminine.

Kings: Selfish, unwise use of power and control, inconstant, weak, absent, unmasculine, bullying, arrogant, overthrowing parental or societal strictures and authority, the inner masculine.

Wands: Too much or little energy or action, selfishness, burn-out.

Cups: Overly emotional or unfeeling, unrealistic or unimaginative, unworldly, addictive, amoral.

Swords: Lacking in compassion or forgiveness, ineffective, indiscriminate, judgmental, unthinking.

Pentacles: Material loss or overindulgence, envy, laziness.

Major Arcana: Unresolved issues, unactualized potential, surrender, seeing beneath the surface, alternate realities, breakthroughs.

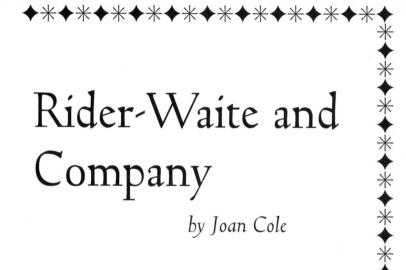

Rider-Waite and Company

by Joan Cole

The *Rider-Waite* deck has apparently become the de facto standard deck for tarot readers, at least in North America. Most tarotists have a basic knowledge of it, and the vast majority of books in English on the subject of tarot are written with this deck in mind. For good or ill, it has become a common vocabulary, such that new students of tarot are quite often told that their first deck should be either "the *Rider-Waite* or a *Rider-Waite* clone."

This is really quite an achievement for a deck that was published in 1909. It doesn't have this position because it's the first tarot deck—not even close: it misses that honor by nearly five hundred years, given that tarot seems to have been invented in the early to mid-fifteenth century. It's not the first deck to have scenic pictures on each card: the fifteenth-century *Sola Busca* deck preceded it by centuries. It's not the first deck that was designed for divination—that would be the deck by Etteilla (1789), the first Egyptianized deck. It's not the first modern occult deck: *De Guaita-Wirth* (1889), *Falconnier-Wegener* (1896), and *Papus-Goulinat* (1909) all came before the *Rider-Waite*. However, it was the first modern occult deck that was produced and made commercially available in Britain.

The deck was illustrated by Pamela Colman-Smith under the instruction of Arthur Edward Waite and published by Rider &

Company. Waite was a Christian mystic and prolific writer on Freemasonry, Rosicrucianism, and other occult subjects. Smith was a trained artist and illustrator who had toured with a theater company doing set and costume design. Her artwork for the deck was a work done for hire, and as a result her name was not prominently associated with the deck. Today many tarotists add her name to the deck in recognition of her contribution, as I do, referring to it as the *Rider-Waite-Smith*, or RWS.

Both Waite and Smith were members of the Hermetic Order of the Golden Dawn. Waite had published the first English translation of Eliphas Lévi and was knowledgeable about the French school of Etteilla, Lévi, Paul Christian, and Papus. As an occult scholar with knowledge of both published (French) sources and secret (Golden Dawn) attributions, he was perfectly placed to design a deck that looked to both traditions. This helps to explain why those of a scholarly bent so love the deck, but not why the deck enjoys overall popularity.

For whatever reason, this deck got wider circulation in the English-speaking world than any other deck for many years. Perhaps as a result, the RWS has been the model used by designers of new decks more than any other deck, and the deck discussed in more tarot books than any other deck. With so many teaching

Death from *The Rider-Waite Tarot*

Death from the *Ship of Fools Tarot*

The Fool from *The Rider-Waite Tarot*

The Fool from *The Fey Tarot*

materials to choose from, it is a safe bet for a beginner to choose a deck in the RWS pattern as a first deck. And there are so many decks in the pattern to choose from that there is a *"Rider-Waite* clone" for nearly any artistic taste.

As tarot scholar James Revak has pointed out, the word "clone" implies an exact copy. So technically, only another RWS deck would be an RWS clone. It is more accurate to call these decks variations, since they retain only some features of the original. Some variations are straightforward and still show substantially the same scenes. These decks would still be reasonably well described in a book written about the RWS. However, there is another group of decks that, while copying a number of features of the RWS, do more than vary the images. Sometimes they are fusions of multiple historical or occult decks. Sometimes they present completely new designs for an entire group of cards. To use a musical analogy, I think these decks are really improvisations rather than variations. If you know the standard the musicians are improvising from, you can recognize it easily. But if you don't, having heard the improvisation won't tell you very much about what it sounds like when it's played straight. It boils down to the degree of similarity: at a certain point, a variation is dissimilar enough that it is its own tune, in addition to being a riff off another. At that point I am calling it an improvisation.

I think this distinction between variations and improvisations is particularly useful for beginners. Beginners should be aware that improvisations, which tend to replace RWS symbols with different symbols, frequently cause confusion when studied in conjunction with a book or class intended for the RWS. But variations, often simply missing symbolism, can be quite suitable, since tarot study typically begins with associating very basic keywords with very basic visual scenes. A beginning tarot class is not going to do an in-depth analysis of all the details of each scene on all seventy-eight cards because it would throw the students into information overload, and such an in-depth analysis won't be found in a beginning tarot book. So even though a variation may be missing quite a bit of symbolism, as long as the basic scene is preserved, RWS learning materials will still be useable.

Looking for a reasonably objective way to rank each deck by degree of similarity to the RWS, I was inspired by Bob O'Neill's use of quantitative iconography. I selected a subset of cards from each part of the deck to analyze, and for each card specified symbolic phrases to look for. If the complete phrase was present, 2 points were awarded; if it was only partially present, 1 point was awarded. For instance, the RWS Lovers card depicts the trees of life and knowledge; the mere presence of two trees in a Lovers card from another deck

The Magician from *The Rider-Waite Tarot*

The Magician from *The Victoria Regina Tarot*

was worth 1 point; the full 2 points required that one tree bore fruit and had a snake, and that the other had flaming foliage. I could expect to find some phrases in any deck variation, while other phrases were very specific and frequently were not found, like the fallen man's hand position on the Ten of Swords. With the notion that a variation should have more than half the searched-for symbolism, I made the cutoff between variation and improvisation at 55 percent of the possible points of similarity, or 35 points.

This is not an exhaustive listing of RWS-inspired decks, but does contain both widely available decks and a few gems currently being self-published by their creators. A wide variety of themes, art styles, and media are included, from black-and-white photography to decks reminiscent of stained-glass windows. In this table, the number of similarity points scored by each deck is shown in parentheses after the rest of the deck information.

Recolored Variations (Images Reproduce the RWS)

Albano-Waite Tarot, Frankie Albano
Diamond Tarot, Klaus Holitzka
Illuminated Tarot, Carol Herzer
Original Rider-Waite Tarot, facsimile
Universal Waite Tarot, Mary Hanson-Roberts

Redrawn Variations

Universal Tarots, Roberto de Angelis (51)
Hanson-Roberts Tarot, Mary Hanson-Roberts (49)
Robin Wood Tarot, Robin Wood (47)
Beginner's Guide to Tarot, Juliet Sharman-Burke and Giovanni Caselli (41)
Mountain Dream Tarot, Bea Nettles (41)
Tarot of the Cloisters, Michelle Leavitt (40)
The New Palladini Tarot, David Palladini (38)
Tarot of Prague, Alexandr Ukolov and Karen Mahony (37)
Morgan-Greer Tarot, William Greer and Lloyd Morgan (36)

Redrawn Variations with a Different Theme

African Tarot, Marina Romito (45)
Mage: The Ascension Tarot, Nicky Rea and Jackie Cassada (44)
Russian Tarot of St Petersburg, Yury Shakov (41)
Hello Tarot!, Joe Rosales (37)

♦ **Improvisations**

Spiral Tarot, Kay Steventon (30)
World Spirit Tarot, Lauren O'Leary (30)
Aquarian Tarot, David Palladini (27)
Hudes Tarot, Susan Hudes (27)
Nigel Jackson Tarot, Nigel Jackson (26)
Light and Shadow Tarot, Michael Goepferd (24)
Gendron Tarot, Melanie Gendron (23)
Londa Tarot, Londa Marks (23)
Melissa Townsend Tarot, Melissa Townsend (19)
Wonderland Tarot, Christopher and Morgana Abbey (33)
Buckland Romani Tarot, Raymond Buckland and Lissanne Lake (32)
Tarot of the Southwest Sacred Tribes, Violeta Monreal (28)
Halloween Tarot, Kipling West (26)
Victoria Regina Tarot, Sarah Ovenall (26)
Xultun Tarot, Pater Balin (26)
Ancestral Path Tarot, Julie Cuccia-Watts (25)
Secret Tarots, Marco Nizzoli (22)

Test the Tarot

by Mark McElroy

Even the most modest psychic fairs feature astrologers, aura photographers, astral projection specialists, crystal vendors, feng shui consultants, reiki healers, mediums in touch with every invisible entity imaginable, intuitives, sensitives, empaths, shamans . . . and, of course, tarot readers.

In fact, there's only one kind of person I don't often meet at psychic fairs: skeptics.

In my work with tarot, though, I meet skeptics every day. When I mention my work with brainstorming, goal setting, and action planning, they are all ears. "How fascinating!" they say. "Please demonstrate!" But when I reveal that I brainstorm, set goals, and plan action using tarot cards, they shift uncomfortably in their seats. "Tarot cards? As in fortunetelling, palm reading—that sort of thing?"

I empathize with that response—after all, I was a skeptic once, myself. When I started toying with the tarot, a part of me didn't want it to work! Ultimately, firsthand experience—and nothing else—convinced me of tarot's value as a creative tool.

Recalling that experience, I started thinking about an experimental approach to tarot deliberately designed with skeptics in mind. I envisioned a Tarot Challenge—a fast, fun, hands-on experience for people who normally wouldn't touch tarot. Here's how it works.

Mention to your most skeptical friends, relatives, and associates that you've come across seven tarot experiments, none of which takes more than fifteen minutes to complete. Say you're curious what might happen if someone with little or no real interest in tarot tried these experiments. Finish with an appeal: "If I gave you the step-by-step instructions and a deck of cards, would you consider contributing fifteen minutes a day for just one week?"

Once they agree, provide them with the twenty-one trumps and the Fool from virtually any tarot deck (I recommend the *Universal Tarot*, the *Robin Wood Tarot*, or some version of the *Rider-Waite-Smith* cards) and the simple instructions found at the end of this article. A week later, talk with them about their experience. What were their preconceptions? How did it feel when they performed the experiments? What worked? What didn't? How has the experience changed the way they see tarot?

When the time comes, accept their feedback without criticism or defensiveness. Some people see patterns, make associations, and draw conclusions very naturally; others do so with great difficulty. Some see what they expect to see; others will be mildly interested. One—perhaps the one you least expect—may thank you for introducing these amazing little cards and say, "How did I ever live without them?"

That said: what are we waiting for? It's time to gather up the trumps from your favorite deck, duplicate the instructions below, find your favorite skeptic . . . and test the tarot!

Test the Tarot

Thanks for agreeing to take the Tarot Challenge! This seven-day program provides a series of seven experiments—one for each day. None of the activities require more than fifteen minutes. After completing them, you'll be one of very few people who, instead of simply dismissing tarot as a tool for creative thinking and reflection, can say, "I know what I'm talking about, because I tried it myself!"

What You Need

The twenty-two "Majors" or trumps from any tarot deck
A pencil
Some paper

Before You Start

Before doing any of the experiments, imagine a scale from 1 to 10, in which:

> 1 means, "I have no desire at all to know about tarot."
> 5 means, "I don't feel one way or the other about tarot."
> 10 means, "I want to learn more about tarot and its uses."

On this scale of 1 to 10, where do you fall today? _____

With that question answered, you are ready to begin.

Day One

Morning: Spend five minutes looking at the cards: their titles, their colors, their images. When done, shuffle them using any method you choose. Pick one facedown card and, without looking at it, set it aside. That's all—until tonight!

Evening: Return to the card you selected this morning, look at it, and do the following:

1) Notice details. Take at least sixty seconds to note as many details as possible.

2) Pick three items. Of all the elements on the card, write down three things that stand out to you. These can be colors, numbers, people, postures, words in the margins, expressions on faces, objects in the background or even an emotion you feel the card seems to suggest. (For example, you might write: "apples, the feeling of curiosity, and the fellow on the left who looks a bit like my Aunt Martha.")

3) Make associations. For each of the three items you noticed, write down three associations—three things from your own experience that "connect" with each item in some way. (For example, if you noticed an apple, you might think of hot apple pie; the color red; and the Bible story about Adam, Eve, the serpent, and the apple.)

There are no wrong answers. Any associations at all will do! Write down any associations you make before answering these questions:

1) Did any of these elements or associations play a role in your day today? If so, which ones? What role did they play?

2) Do you associate any of these elements or associations with people you met with or talked to today? If so, with whom? How are they associated?

3) Did anything happen today that you didn't plan on or expect? If so, do any of these elements or associations relate to that unexpected event?

4) Is there another card in the deck you feel better reflects your day? If so, which would it be and why?

Day Two

Morning: Again, shuffle the cards and choose one—but today, look at your card. Just as you did yesterday, note three items that stand out to you. Write these down, along with three associations for each.

Evening. Below is a list of themes associated with each of the cards. Find your card in the list and read its theme, then answer tonight's questions.

0 – Fool: Beginnings, carelessness, open-mindedness

I – Magician: Lightning, inspiration, getting your way

II – High Priestess: Dreams, daydreams, virginity, imagination

III - Empress: Pregnancy, babies, productivity, teaching

IV – Emperor: Giving orders, taking charge, fighting

V – Hierophant: Church, spirituality, guiding, authority

VI – Lovers: Romance, reunion, making things complete

VII – Chariot: Winning, speed, being a hero, achieving a goal

VIII – Strength: Physical strength, self-discipline, direction

IX – Hermit: Being alone, withdrawing, holding back, wisdom

X – Wheel: Chance, luck, birthdays, anniversaries, repetition

XI – Justice: Law, rules, restrictions, making tough decisions

XII – Hanged Man: Traitors, a new perspective, lessons learned

XIII – Death: Endings, transitions, changes, conclusions

XIV – Temperance: Blending, being moderate, being careful

XV – Devil: Greed, materialism, addiction, physical pleasure

XVI – Tower: Disruption, shake-ups, sudden changes

XVII – Star: Hope, setting goals, honest responses

XVIII – Moon: Rapid change, passion, getting wild, letting loose

IXX – Sun: Celebration, warmth, openness, truth, freedom

XX – Judgment: Waking to possibilities, sudden excitement

XXI - World: Having it all, completeness, happiness

1) If you had to say this card "means something," what would you say it means? Does your answer match or conflict with the table above? (Either way, you're okay.)

2) Did your selected items or associations play a role in your day? If so, how?

3) Did the theme or meaning of your card play a role in your day? If so, how?

Day Three

Morning: As you have done previously, shuffle the cards, select one, identify three elements that capture your attention, and come up with three associations for each of those elements. Once done, read the theme of your card as it appears in the chart provided on Day Two, and then answer the following questions:

1) What one-word emotion do you associate with this card?

2) What moment from your past could be associated with this card?

3) Imagine this card tells you about an opportunity coming your way today. What opportunity might this card be telling you to watch for?

For example: if you draw the Hierophant, you might write:

1) Seriousness

2) The time a minister helped with a school project

3) Watch for an opportunity to help others

Evening: Tonight, review your answers from this morning, then answer the following questions:

1) At some point during the day, did you feel the emotion you defined earlier? What were the circumstances?

2) Did anything happen today that connected to or reminded you of the memory you recalled this morning?

3) Did the opportunity you imagined come about in some way? If so, how?

Day Four

Morning: Pick out a specific event, task, or interaction that you know will take place today. (A meeting, perhaps, or a conversation with a coworker.) When you've selected something, write it down.

With this in mind, shuffle the cards and draw one. Pretend this card is a message about the moment you selected, expressed as a picture. Imagine the message is "To make [the moment you selected] as smooth and pleasant as possible, you should [do this]."

Inspired by the card, fill in the [do this] blank with something you might actually do or say. Write it down—and, when the moment comes later today, put this advice into action.

Evening: Did you try the advice you generated this morning? If not, why not? If so, what was the outcome? Did you see the event, task, or interaction differently as a result of working with your card?

Day Five

Morning: Shuffle the cards and draw one. Pretend this card is a coded message just for you, saying, "To make today a better day, [do this]." (If you need to, refer to the chart of themes from Day Three for ideas, or use the association process to prompt some ideas.) What would the message be? Write down your answer.

Evening: Did you take an action today based on the "message" you received from the card? If not, why not? If so, how did things go? Did the day get better?

Day Six

Morning: Consider the question, "What's something I can do today that will make me feel more productive?" Draw a single card. Based on this card, come up with three recommendations for action that would make you feel more productive. (For example, because you associate the Chariot with your car, with speed, and winning, you might write, "Get the car serviced. Get the house cleaned as quickly as possible. Buy a lottery ticket."

When you have your three recommendations in mind, write them down. During the day, put them into action.

Evening: How many of your ideas did you put into action? What were the results? Now that the day is over, how do you feel about it?

Day Seven

Morning: Shuffle the deck and draw two cards. Pretend the first card describes how you felt about tarot at the beginning of our experiment, and that the second describes how your feelings have changed. With the cards in mind, finish these sentences:

1) When this started, I felt _____.

2) Now that this is almost over, I feel _____.

Evening: If this week's experiments went well, you've seen for yourself how the cards can help you reflect on your experiences, come up with new ideas, anticipate potential issues, and plan your day. To cap things off, please write down the answer to this question:

Imagine a scale from 1 to 10, where:

1 means, "I don't want to know anything else about tarot."
5 means, "I'm completely neutral about tarot."
10 means, "I'd like to find out more about tarot."

On this scale of 1 to 10, where do you fall today? _____

Compare this answer to the answer you gave at the beginning of the experiment . . . and be sure to share your answers with the friend who passed these instructions to you!

The Magician

Practical Applications

IL MAGO
LE BATELEUR

THE MAGICIAN
EL MAGO

DER MAGIER

DE MAGIËR

Finding Your Voice

by Nina Lee Braden

What is it about you as a tarot reader that is unique? What is it about you as a tarot reader that separates you from other tarot readers? What is your special talent or gift as a tarot reader? Are you empathic? Are you extremely focused? Have you studied the tarot long and deep? Are you gifted intuitively? Everyone has a special talent that helps him or her in reading the tarot.

We all have a past, which also affects how we read tarot. What was your spiritual path as you grew up? This will influence how you read tarot. What did you study in school? This will influence how you read tarot. What are your hobbies and special interests? These will influence how you read tarot. You bring to a tarot reading the sum total of who you are and what you have learned, and we are all uniquely different in this regard.

No tarot reader has ever been able to read well for everyone. Some tarot readers are good at reading for a very diverse clientele, and other tarot readers have a more limited client base. None of us can please, reach, help, and connect with everyone. Just as no writer, no matter how great, will appeal to everyone. Shakespeare couldn't do it, Jane Austen couldn't do it, and even Walt Whitman (my personal favorite) couldn't do it. No one tarot reader can effectively reach every querent either, although there are techniques and tools that can increase our abilities to be effective with more people.

Perhaps the first step to becoming a good tarot reader is to have a solid knowledge of tarot. However, knowing tarot is not enough to make you a good tarot reader. That would be like saying that having a good vocabulary is enough to make you a good writer. It just isn't so. Having a good vocabulary is an excellent asset for a writer, but a writer needs more than that. Knowing tarot is essential for a tarot reader, but it is not enough.

Let's begin by looking at who we are as individuals. Our personal strengths and weaknesses affect how we read. An extrovert will read differently than an introvert will. An intense person will read differently than a laid-back person will. A person with a wacky sense of humor will read differently than someone who is more serious. So, know thyself. Take a serious and thorough self-inventory of your strengths and weaknesses as a human being and as a communicator.

How do we take knowing ourselves in general and apply it to knowing ourselves as readers? We can do several things. If you know astrology, you can look at your natal chart. In a person's natal chart, the Sun, Moon, and Ascendant are always important. Everything else has to work with those components. However, counseling or advising is associated with the Seventh House in astrology. Look at the sign on the cusp of your Seventh House. This should tell you something about your reading style. Are there any planets in your Seventh House? If so, this will make a difference. Every sign has a planet as a natural ruler. What planet rules the sign on your Seventh House? Where is that planet? What sign is it in? These can all be useful aids in helping to determine your strengths and weaknesses as a reader.

For example, I am a Scorpio Sun with a Leo Moon and a Cancer Ascendant. I am an intense person who needs to simultaneously nurture and to be the center of attention. This is why I like teaching and public speaking. It allows me to be intense, to be the center of attention, and to help other people all at the same time. This astrological description of me as a person will carry over to my reading style. In addition, I have Capricorn on the cusp of my Seventh House. This means that any counseling I do will tend to be very practical. I will be very logical. I will want my counseling sessions to yield some sort of goal or ambition or "take charge" attitude on behalf of my client. I will want to empower my client to be able to go out and achieve great things. Saturn is the planet that rules Capricorn, and, natally, I have Saturn in Scorpio in the Fifth House. Readings with me will tend to be intense, but they'll also be entertaining and fun. They will be creative (Fifth House) yet utilitarian (Saturn). Because of Saturn, sometimes a reading with me will feel like hard work for both me and my client.

In addition, if you know numerology, runes, I-Ching, or any other divinatory methods, you can use them to help you figure out your natural talents and strengths as a reader. Finally, you can use the tarot itself. You can use the cards associated with your astrological chart. You can use your Personality and Soul cards. You can even do a reading based on the question, "How might I best utilize my natural gifts as a reader?"

Here is a simple three-card spread that you could use to help you find your voice as a reader.

Card One: My strengths as a reader.
Card Two: My weaknesses as a reader.
Card Three: The tension or dynamic between my strengths and my weaknesses that allows me to be most creative.

Finally, using writing as an example, we could take the input of our metaphysical tools, plus our own thoughts, and brainstorm. We could do free-form writing. When brainstorming or freewriting, we don't censor our thoughts. We just let the ideas flow and write them down. We could also use other prewriting techniques such as listing, clustering, or outlining. We could journal or dialogue with a trusted friend.

When we are done with all of this discovery, we should have learned a lot about ourselves as individuals and as readers. However, self-discovery is only the first stage. We must take this

Strengths	Weaknesses	Tension

self-knowledge and temper it like an alchemist in search of the philosopher's stone. We distill the essence of what we hope to accomplish in our readings into one golden sentence. In writing, we call this our thesis.

What is your thesis of reading? What is your goal? What do you want to accomplish? How do you want to accomplish it? Distill this further into a persona. Who are you as reader? Are you a:

Coach	Mother
Teacher	Guide
Best Friend	Psychologist
Surgeon	Social Worker
Police Officer	Mentor
Minister	Shaman
Walker between Worlds	Scout
Storyteller	Interpreter
Intermediary	Reporter
Judge	Fisher
Bridge-builder	Witness
Truth-teller	Channeler of the Divine
Mirror	Plumber
Cheerleader	Treasure Hunter
Pioneer	Sybil
Prophet	Healer
Dream-catcher	Medicine Woman/Man
Facilitator	Midwife of the Soul
Tool Giver	Editor
Excavator	Dealer in Possibilities

Test your persona against several problem situations. For example, if you are a scout, how would you, as a scout, handle a skeptical client? How would you handle a client who was swallowed by self-defeat? How would you handle a reading where you had a conflict of interest? How would you handle the perennial seeker who goes from one reader to another until she finally hears what she wants to hear? If you read as a best friend, how would you handle these situations? If you read as a storyteller? As a minister? As a judge?

After testing your persona against some problematic readings, you may want to rethink and revise your approach. In other words, you may think that your best style or persona is one style, but as

you test it you may find that you are really more comfortable using
a slightly different style. You may also find that you combine two
or three different approaches. You'll have a primary approach, but
also a secondary one, and possibly a tertiary one. I find that I read
primarily as a guide, but I'm also strongly a teacher. Occasionally,
I'll also read as a minister. For me, these three work well together.

In writing, we call this "finding your voice" or "finding your
style." Jane Austen doesn't write like Shakespeare, nor does she
need to. Shakespeare's voice is different from Tennessee Williams's
voice. Tennessee Williams's style is different from Toni Morrison's
style. Toni Morrison's voice is different from Emily Dickinson's.
Each of these writers is very versatile, very gifted, but each has a
unique voice, so that even when you are reading an unfamiliar
quote, you can say, "This sounds like Shakespeare," or, "This
sounds like Emily Dickinson," and you'll be right. You can recognize the voice even when you don't recognize the words.

Have you ever heard a new song on the radio, but you didn't
hear the DJ announce the singer? Yet, even without hearing the
name of the artist who sings the song, by listening to the artist's
unique voice you've been able to identify the performer. Similarly,

we can often even identify influences on performers. For example, if you listen to Harry Connick, Jr., it is obvious that he is influenced as a singer by Frank Sinatra.

This influence in style can be seen in us as readers. For example, in my readings, although I am my own unique self, reading as a Scorpio Sun/Leo Moon/Cancer Ascendant guide/teacher/minister, I show the influence of James Wanless, Mary Greer, and Rachel Pollack. Anyone who is familiar with the work of these people will see their influence upon me as a reader. Who has influenced you as a reader? Whom would you like to be influenced by? Focus on good readers whose voices you would like to incorporate into your own style. We become more like whatever we focus on. Choose carefully where you place your focus.

So, in review, know yourself. Know your reading strengths and weaknesses. Know your reading style and persona, and realize that no matter what that style or persona is, it needs to be flexible and adaptable enough to handle a wide range of reading situations.

Once you've found your voice, you'll be better able to target your audience as well. Just as you may have a primary, secondary, and tertiary voice, you may find that you have a primary, secondary, and tertiary audience.

Someone who reads as a coach is going to attract a different clientele than someone who reads as a mother. Someone who reads as a shaman is going to attract a different clientele than someone who reads as a storyteller. One is not better than another, but one may be better for a certain client than the other. As beginning readers, we often have a lot of mismatches between our reading styles and our audience. As we gain experience and reputation as readers, the number of mismatches grows fewer.

No matter where we are in our development as readers, we can improve our voices. We can continue to grow as readers. We can continue to learn about ourselves, about humanity in general, and about the tarot itself. Each new discovery that we make is reflected in our voices. Let us all strive for rich, multilayered voices; voices which sing with power, grace, and warmth; voices which are supple and flexible; voices which shine with our own unique persona; and voices which also transparently allow the magic of the tarot to color our lives and the lives of those around us.

Note: This article is based on a presentation given at the Readers Studio in New York City in April 2003.

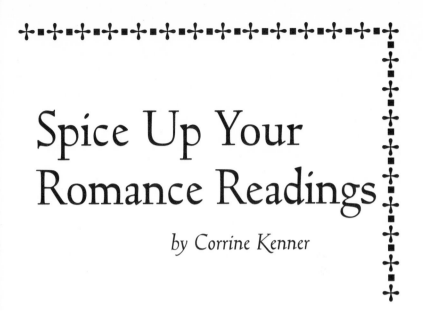

Spice Up Your Romance Readings

by Corrine Kenner

A young woman sits across from you, quietly weeping. She wipes her nose and studies the cards on the table. No matter how hard she searches, however, there are no Knights in the spread to ride to her rescue. There are no cooing Lovers, no toasting couple in the Two of Cups, and no newlyweds dancing in the Four of Wands. The spread consists mainly of a few lonely looking individuals, all gathered around a broken-hearted Three of Swords—and the sight of that rainy, pain-filled card makes your client cry even more.

It's a typical romance reading—and for many tarot readers, it's all too predictable.

"Everyone wants to know about love," one professional tarot reader said at a recent conference. "And every reading is the same: 'When will I meet someone? Will I get married? Is my lover faithful?' It just gets boring after a while."

If you feel weepy at the prospect of another romance reading, it's time to find a few new ways to put the spark back in your reading routine.

Set the Right Mood
First, make sure you're working in an atmosphere that's conducive

to romance readings. If you're not in the mood to talk about love, you can recharge your reading space with a few simple accessories.

Start with your spread cloth. Of course, your black silk scarf is traditional, but it's not exactly energizing. Fold it up and replace it with something unmistakably symbolic of love and romance—a red satin pillowcase, for example. You could go a step further and spread your cards on the weddings and engagements page of your local newspaper. For an even more dramatic presentation, you could actually spread your cards on an evening gown, a wedding dress, or a flowing bridal veil.

Keep your eyes open for other accessories that can help set the mood for a romance reading. Scatter a few rose petals on the table and scent the air with perfume. Collect some tokens that symbolize an evening out—like movie tickets or a restaurant menu. Decorate your reading space with the bride and groom from the top of a wedding cake.

Use the cards themselves for inspiration. To symbolize the fiery passions of the Wands cards, light several candles. To symbolize the watery emotions of the suit of Cups, serve champagne or sparkling cider in elegant crystal flutes. To symbolize the airy communications of the Swords cards, display a volume of romantic poetry, a collection of Valentine's Day cards, or a few elegantly scripted love letters—even if you have to write them yourself. And to symbolize the physical pleasures of the Pentacles, share a few chocolates as you contemplate the cards.

Also, plan to involve your clients by asking them to add a romantic token of their own to the spread: a note, a phone number, or a piece of jewelry. If your client happens to have a photo of himself or herself with the loved one in question, use it as the significator card.

While romantic objects and accessories can add excitement to your reading space, you can also spice up your sessions by adding more substance to the romance readings themselves.

Ask Questions

If romance readings turn you off, do an about-face and shift your focus from the readings to the questions. You might even plan to spend more time exploring the questions than the answers.

Naturally, most readings begin with a question, but most queries usually take just a minute or two to get out. Moreover, typical romance readings tend to focus on a few tried-and-true inquiries, such as "Who loves me?" "When will I find love?" or "Do I have a soul mate?"

As strange as it sounds, however, those questions really aren't questions at all. Rather, they simply represent each client's thinly veiled hopes and dreams for a better future. Each client's question, after all, is actually a quest in disguise. Once you discover which quest your client is on, you can develop a query that will elicit a clear and specific response.

First, ask each client what he or she would like to know from the cards. Then develop that question fully—initially, by asking for background information. You might ask your clients the reason for their inquiries. You might ask about the circumstances that have led up to the reading. You could even ask questioners about the answers they think they'll hear, and then compare those to the answers they actually hope to receive.

Next, help your client refine and rephrase that original question in light of the new information you've developed. Avoid questions that might elicit yes-or-no answers. Rather than asking, "Will I find love?" for example, you'll get more insight—and more information—from related questions like, "What do I have to offer a partner?" "What do I want from a relationship?" "What should I expect from a relationship?" "How can I be more attractive to prospective partners?" "What should I do to find a partner?" "Where should I look for love?" "How can I be ready for love?" and, of course, "How can I be happily single in the meantime?"

Consult the Court Cards

For many tarot readers, it's all too easy to think of the court cards simply as facets of a client's personality or as projections of other people in your client's life. There is far more to the court cards than meets the eye, however. In fact, the court cards are the embodiment of family matters, partnerships, and marriages. The court cards are the de facto relationship experts of the tarot deck—and they can become your allies in conducting romance readings.

You might want to base your next romance reading on this innovative, courts-only spread. First, pull the sixteen court cards out and set the rest of the deck aside. Shuffle them, and deal them into two rows of four cards each. The first row will represent your client's strengths—the gifts and talents he or she brings to relationships. The second row will represent your client's weaknesses—or, to be more tactful, the areas in which he or she has room to improve.

The four cards in each row will each relate to the four suits of the Minor Arcana. The first card in each row will represent spiritual gifts, which are usually represented by the fiery suit of Wands. The second card in each row will represent emotional affairs, which typically correspond to the watery suit of Cups. The third card in each row will represent intellectual issues, like the airy suit of Swords. The fourth card in each row will embody physical matters, the realm of the earthy suit of Pentacles.

Turn over the cards one by one, and assess each one in terms of its traditional significance along with its place in the spread. Pages, for example, symbolize youth, enthusiasm, and an unbounded capacity to learn; they are students and messengers. If the first card in the first row is the Page of Wands, for example, you would be correct in saying that your client has a gift for developing the spiritual side of a relationship.

Likewise, Knights are adventurers, eager to embark on sacred quests, defend the helpless, and rescue those in jeopardy. Queens are mature women, gracious and wise in the ways of the world, and ready to safeguard and nurture those in their realms. Kings are seasoned, experienced men who have successfully completed the quests they began as knights. They have grown to become authoritative rulers and strong protectors.

Naturally, you won't necessarily find that a Wands card has fallen in a "Wands" position, or that any of the cards fall into their corresponding places in the spread. If a card does fall in its own realm, however, you can probably be assured that the traits associated with it are clear cut and well defined.

Be Selective

If you've done tarot readings for any length of time, you've probably noticed that people who want romance readings are frequently unhappy with their love lives. Their relationships are failing, broken, or nonexistent, and they find themselves at a dead end.

Tarot cards, with their vivid imagery and countless combinations of cards, offer a versatile, useful tool for helping your clients envision and prepare for a brighter, better future.

Traditionally, tarot readers have consulted the cards by shuffling and dealing the cards facedown. The cards fall as they will, and a questioner's fate hangs on the luck of the draw. Until each card in a spread is turned faceup, no one knows what secrets or truths the cards will reveal.

However, there is no rule that says the cards must be dealt facedown. In fact, it can be just as instructional, insightful, and intuitive to let your clients choose the cards they want to appear in the spread. It's a radical technique, which I call a selective reading, and it's designed to put all of the cards in your client's hands—literally.

The process is an extension of what tarot expert James Wanless terms fortune creation, rather than fortune telling. It's active, not passive. It's optimistic and enlightening, and in many ways it's more interesting than readings that rely upon the luck of the draw.

The method itself is simple—but it's intense. You can use it with any spread, from a basic Past-Present-Future layout to the more complex Celtic Cross, but rather than shuffling and spreading the cards yourself, hand the whole deck to your client. Then ask your client to look through all seventy-eight cards, and choose one card for each position in the spread.

During a selective reading, your role will be more of a guide than a reader. It will be your job to direct your client—first by describing the significance each position in the spread, and then by explaining the symbolism and traditional interpretation of each card. Most of your clients will probably find two or three cards that might fit in each position. Your role will be to help them narrow their choice to a single card.

You might be surprised at how easy it is for your clients to select appropriate cards—especially when choosing cards to represent the past. Old patterns of behavior are very recognizable in the images of the cards, and it's easy to be honest when they're dealing with a neutral third party like the tarot. Moreover, by helping your clients clarify in their own hearts and their own minds what they want most, you'll help them be better prepared to spot new opportunities, people, and possibilities.

Keep the Kleenex Handy

Ultimately, romance readings will always be emotional affairs. The lovelorn and the broken-hearted will always find their way to a tarot-reader's table.

With a few changes in your accessories and your attitude, however, your romance readings can make your clients weep for joy—not sadness—and you'll find that each session is good for you, too.

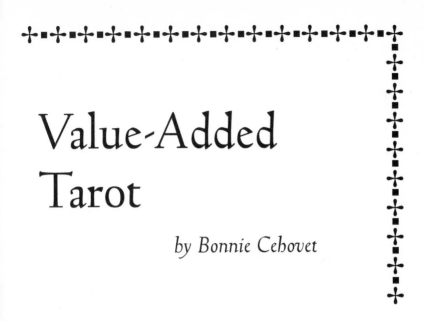

Value-Added Tarot

by Bonnie Cehovet

When we look at tarot as a business, we are actually looking at several different layers of definition. One layer is that of tarot reading: the business consists of giving tarot readings, no more, no less. Another layer is that of teaching the tarot, which often comes as an offshoot of giving tarot readings. Yet another layer is that of consulting, whether it's in a client's private life, spiritual life, or career. This then becomes the "business" of tarot—tarot taken to the professional level.

As with any business venture, tarot professionals are faced with bringing in new business, encouraging repeat business, and "branding" themselves to encourage word-of-mouth clients. One of the ways to accomplish this is through the concept of "added value." Added value means that the client receives something of value—whether an added service or a physical object—that is free. What the tarot professional determines to be acceptable as added value depends on the nature of the business, the environment (i.e. what is generally accepted in the area where the business is located) and the tools that he or she is comfortable working with.

What does the tarot professional receive in return for adding value to his or her business? New clients come in, existing clients become repeat business, and "word of mouth" becomes a magical elixir! On a more personal level, while in the process of "branding," or defining themselves, tarot professionals expand their own understanding of what tarot is and how it can be used, and they learn to combine the tools at their command. The gift of added value is twofold: the clients feel that they have received something over and above what they paid for, and the tarot professionals feel that they have ways of growing their businesses that cost them next to nothing. Everybody wins here!

Tapes

Let's take a look at some of the ways that we can add value to our tarot businesses. The first situation that we will look at is the tarot professional who functions as a reader. The first thing that I did with my business was to offer a free tape of the reading. I never even consciously thought of this as added value—I simply thought that was what one did, as I had always received tapes when I was read for by others. The gift of a tape of the reading allows the client to review what he or she was told—which is very important, as most readings tend to be emotionally charged. There is a second level of added value with the gift of a tape which came out in a tele-conference class that I did on added value. Someone pointed out that there are many different types of labels for audio cassettes (and yes—I had been using the ones that came with the tape!). Labels are available in different colors, and can be imprinted with business information such as the name, address, and phone number of the business; the name of the reader; or anything that the reader feels creates a professional identity.

Crystals

Working with crystals is something that comes naturally to me, and it was a perfect fit for my tarot practice. I place a pretty dish containing rose quartz crystals in the reading area. After they have shuffled the cards, I ask my clients to pick one or two of the crystals to hold during the reading. I give them a little of the background of the rose quartz—its healing properties and the fact that it will hold the memory of the reading for them. I let them know before I begin reading that the crystals are theirs to take with them. This allows me to create a personal bond with my clients, and takes the edge off of their nervousness.

Crystals can be used as a gift of wisdom after the reading. You can keep a range of crystals handy that deal with specific issues that come out during a reading. Clients are then gifted with the crystals that will help them deal with their personal issues. Examples here might be: abundance/prosperity (citrine, jade, smoky quartz, turquoise), grounding/centering (agate, Apache tears, hematite), healing (amazonite, amber, amethyst, rose quartz), psychic protection (azurite, blue lace agate, clear quartz). The cost of the crystals is not great, but the benefit to the client is.

Numerology

A wonderful way to create a clear connection with your clients before beginning a reading is to combine the art of tarot with the art of numerology. By using the numbers from the birthdate, one or two (depending on the system used) birth cards are created. Basically the numbers are added together until a number of twenty-one or less is obtained (the Fool is not used in this process). The Major Arcana card that matches the birth card number is the tarot birth card. For example, if the client's birth data added up to the number six, the corresponding Major Arcana card would be the Lovers. This card represents the theme for this lifetime. It is helpful to draw this card from a separate deck than that which is to be used for the reading itself. I tend to place the card above the reading and to one side, so that it is there for both my client and myself to use as a visual reference.

Another method for using tarot and numerology is to create a tarot profile. Choosing several different categories (i.e., personal day, personal month, personal year, and/or personal challenge), the tarot professional works up a presentation that can be printed

out and discussed with the client at the end of the reading. This not only adds value to the reading but creates a very nice way of tying it together and bringing it to a close.

Role-Playing

At times, the cards within a spread may be difficult for a client to understand, or to place in his or her life. If this seems to be the case with one of your clients, ask him or her to pick the one card that he or she most relates to from the reading, and the one card that gives him or her the most discomfort. Starting with the card the client is least comfortable with, take a moment to discuss it. Ask why the client feels uncomfortable with it. Then have the client take the same position that the figure in the card is taking, and talk through the feelings that position brings up. Have the client return to a normal, seated position, and go through the same procedure with the card that he or she most relates to. Then have the client assume the position of the character in the "uncomfortable" card, and walk him or her through moving from that position to the position in the "comfortable" card. As a courtesy to your client, making the movements with him or her will take the edge off of any nervousness, and creates a great reader/client bond.

Affirmations

Affirmations are a tool that come naturally from a reading. At the end of readings, ask your clients about the issues they would most like to take action on. Explain what an affirmation is, and how they work. Spend a few minutes with your clients writing an affirmation that reflects where they are now, what they got out of the reading, and where they want to go.

Teaching

For the tarot professional who chooses to teach, there are other added-value options. One option is a resource list for tarot study. This not only gives your students options for study, but it brings them back to you as the instructor—with questions and new areas that they want to investigate.

An audiotape or a CD that acts as a guided visualization for a
journey into the cards would be most appreciated. The tape should
be very basic, so that it can be used for all of the cards. A work-
sheet to go with it might include areas for who or what your clients
see, predominant smells they encounter, sounds they hear, conversations they might have with the figures, colors they experience,
the landscapes they see, and how they feel in general after step-
ping out of the card.

Ritual

If, as a tarot professional, you are comfortable helping your clients
to "create" the life that they want, then working with ritual is an
option for you. At the end of readings, if it is clear that your clients
have issues that they need to release, or that they have discovered
the energy that they wish to bring into their lives, or if they have
reached some type of milestone that they wish to honor, then helping them to create personal rituals is certainly a value-added
option. Advise them as to the timing of the rituals (in general, the
New Moon is used for bringing things in, or for new beginnings; the
Full Moon is used for releasing issues). Help your clients to focus
on the intent of the rituals and what they want to say. Discuss the
"little things"—the inclusion of music, flowers, incense, candles,
etc. Find out whether they want to work indoors or outdoors, and
if other people will be involved. Set time limits on the discussions,
as you are really just getting your clients started and the rituals are
theirs to build. Both you and your clients will end up feeling very
positive about the time that you spent together—which is what
readings are really all about!

Online and In Print

The tarot professional who opts for an Internet site also has many
unique opportunities to add value to his or her business. One of the
primary ways that a professional can do this is through site content. Personally written articles on the tarot or tarot deck and book
reviews certainly add value. Free site downloads—perhaps a new
tarot spread; an in-depth article; or a chart reflecting astrological,
esoteric, or other correspondences—would get the attention of
those wanting to study tarot (and also might pique the attention of
the nontarot public looking for a tarot reader).

Meditations or affirmations, along with an article on how they
can be put to best use, provide a good source for added value. You

might even choose to put these out in the form of, or as a part of, a free tarot-related newsletter online or in print. This keeps your name in the tarot "public" eye and helps to define you as a reader and as a tarot professional.

Value-Added Tarot

You have opted to become a tarot professional, doing readings, lifestyle counseling, or teaching—or a combination of all three. You have defined who you are as a reader, where you want your business to go, and what your client base will be. You have wrestled with the issue of charging for a reading and have decided on a fee structure. You have a personal code of ethics, understand your local laws regarding tarot reading as a service, and perhaps have even decided to become certified. Now you take yourself to the next level—that of building your business. Look to your strengths, look to the tools that you feel comfortable using. You will put your business on a solid professional foundation by using value-added components that (a) actually do add value to your readings, (b) reflect the values of your community and your clients, and (c) are based on areas in which you are comfortable and well versed.

My wish for each of you is continued success, a sense of personal satisfaction from your work, and that who you are shines through loud and clear as you walk your personal path through life.

The Four-Week Forecast Spread

by Elizabeth Hazel

This forecasting spread provides a quick week-by-week summary, and can be used in a variety of ways. After working with this spread for several months, it has proven most productive when done at the New Moon, with the four three-card segments representing the quarters of the twenty-eight–day lunar cycle. However, it can also be done at the beginning of a calendar month with good results. Some may wish to use this spread as part of a monthly New Moon ritual.

To begin the spread, concentrate on the chosen coming cycle (lunar or calendrical). Shuffle the cards and spread them into the format shown below. Each seven-day period is represented by three cards. The central thirteenth card represents the querent, and indicates how the influences of each week will be understood and processed by the inner self. In order to get the greatest benefit from this spread, transcribe the cards for each week in a datebook or calendar for handy reference.

Interpreting The Forecast

This spread is specifically for mundane (external, worldly) forecasting. It can be used to speculate on personal activities, on business transactions, on family situations, and on weather and other

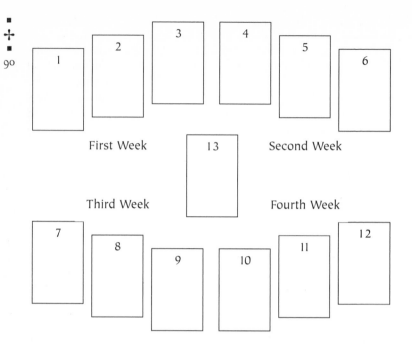

First Week   Second Week

Third Week   Fourth Week

environmental conditions. The cards will suggest which areas of life will be an active focus of attention for the entire period. This style of reading is concerned with the trappings of daily life, so the cards should be interpreted literally. Court cards (Kings, Queens, Knights, and Pages) represent the people one will encounter during the time period, and pip cards (Ace through Ten) will show situations. Unless a card is actually of a meditative nature (like the Seven of Cups) it should be assumed that the cards symbolize external factors during the time period.

Begin the interpretation by focusing on the suits that appear in the weekly segments. Notice whether any suit dominates a trio. A predominance of **Wands** suggests heightened activity, travel, and a swift flow of messages with immediate results. If two or three cards in a weekly segment are Wands, there will be extra pressure to achieve certain goals during that week. Tempers might be high, or friction may occur between individuals whose goals clash. The King and Queen of Wands suggest responsibility for leadership or encouraging others, whereas the Knight and Page indicate participation in team activities, working toward a goal with a group, sporting events, or other collective efforts that center on fun and creativity.

Cups bring a focus on personal exchanges that relate to family, intimacy, and relationships with close friends. This includes social events and domestic tasks: cooking, cleaning, and shopping for food and clothing. The more favorable cards of this suit—the Three, Six, or Nine of Cups for instance—show opportunities for good shopping deals, sales, or discounts on needed items. This potential is increased if all three cards in a weekly segment are Cups. Shop until you drop! The court cards indicate shared confidences, and the specific court card will indicate from whom the confidence will be received. Surrounding cards will indicate whether the information given is public or secret.

Swords indicate the relative speed (or lack of it) in incidents that occur during the week. The Three or Eight of Swords indicate uncomfortable waiting periods. This suit will also show the level of complexity of any communications that occur. The higher the card number, the more complex the situation will be. Two or three Sword cards in a weekly segment indicate that intense thought will be demanded, puzzles solved, or mysteries considered—and that time management is crucial. If a Sword suit card (Ace through Ten) appears next to any court card, it will show whether that individual will be effective in accomplishing necessary tasks or if his or her aims will be confounded by a lack of information, resources, or needed support. The King and Queen of Swords are both powerful cards that indicate a need to carefully analyze what is available to accomplish goals, as well as a mandate to organize and prepare during the time period. The Knight of Swords brings turning points in current situations—perhaps new ideas are being suggested, or a participant enters or leaves. The Page of Swords requires close attention to what is being said by others. Sometimes it is gossip of dubious accuracy, but occasionally the information transmitted is critical to future efforts or brings important clues about opportunities that should not be missed.

Pentacles concentrate on material goods, financial status, and transactions. Underlying this general focus, Pentacles show how secure people are feeling in their situation, or their propensity for worry and anxiety. The Five and Seven of Pentacles indicate complex issues that may require a great deal of time to resolve. If either of these two cards appears at the beginning of the forecast period, the issues indicated may require the entire forecast period to resolve. Feelings of safety and security tend to be generated by the environment and the people in it. The Pentacle cards drawn will indicate if this is reliant on inner stability or dependent on others, particularly in money matters. Generally, the appearance of Pentacle court cards is supportive in nature: these cards are characterized with stable, consistent behavior. The King and Queen of this suit are decisive and managerial, and indicate significant financial transactions, purchases, and the maintenance of personal property. The Knight of Pentacles shows hard work and the need to remain dedicated and focused to complete tasks. The Page suggests learning and study, paperwork, and little practical daily matters that must be attended to in order to keep life flowing smoothly.

Trump cards show major issues, events, or conditions that dominate or change the flow of events during the week. Again, since this spread is concerned with mundane matters, a trump card that appears in a trio should be interpreted in a literal fashion. Some of the trump cards are personified, like the Fool, the Emperor, etc. Read these as individuals dealing with specific issues that have a major impact on the time period—for example, the Emperor could be interpreted as a man dealing with legal concerns or parenting issues. The trump cards that are more conceptual in nature, like Justice or the Tower, will represent events or incidents centered on a specific issue. The Justice card, for instance, shows a critical choice that will dominate the week, perhaps centered on partners or formal agreements. The Tower suggests untoward disruptions that change the flow of the week. The Star can mean stargazing on a clear night, doing divination, going to see a new movie or a concert, or conversations about future plans.

The Center Card

The final, thirteenth card, placed in the center of the spread, represents the querent. This card is interpreted with a nonmundane, inner view. The nature of the card may suggest a proper attitude to maintain during the time period, a personal conflict or a specific goal that encompasses the cycle, or a state of mind that evolves.

If the central card is a trump card, the querent will have a profound influence on his or her surroundings during the month as specifically suggested by the designation of the trump card. The querent will embody the role indicated by the card. For instance, the Devil card in the central position alludes to playing "devil's advocate" during the time period, questioning the practicality of other people's ideas and plans. The Judgment card in the central position shows that the querent is where the "buck stops," and is required to consider long-term consequences and then enforce the resulting decision. If a Page is in one of the surrounding trios, the querent may simply have to put his or her foot down regarding the behavior of a child, but if the King of Wands appears in one of the weekly trios then the querent may have a major decision about initiating an entrepreneurial enterprise that involves a great deal of time, money, and personnel.

A court card in the center is more easily interpreted, because the querent will assume the qualities and characteristics indicated by the card. Kings are paternal and authoritative, Queens are maternal and organizing, Knights are participants and tend to play a supporting role, and Pages are focused on new endeavors and delivering messages. The Kings and Queens require a higher level of confidence and maturity than the Knights and Pages, whereas the Knights and Pages indicate a greater level of flexibility, cooperation, and team spirit. The Wands are enthusiastic, the Cups are compassionate and sensitive, the Swords are skeptical and questioning, and the Pentacles will concentrate on the practical considerations and costs.

Pip cards (Ace through Ten) have broader interpretations when drawn as a central card. A pip card's meaning will evolve during the forecast period, as will the role or state of mind suggested by the divinatory meaning, number and suit element. The small pips (Ace through Three) indicate new situations that will gain momentum during the time period. The middle pips (Four through Six) represent ongoing situations that will need improvement or "tweaking" during the forecast period. The final pips (Seven through Ten) indicate situations that are moving toward resolution. Look for same-suit cards in the surrounding trios for each week. These cards will show when the topic presented by a central pip card will be in development. Notice whether these same-suit cards indicate progress, new developments, confounding delays, or complications. Another clue comes from the other cards in the trio: determine whether these support or hinder the same-suit card.

Comprehensive Indicators

Examine the entire spread for dominant elements. Numbers are one clue to the overall activities of the time period. Any number that appears repeatedly should be considered a key influence, and interpreted with its numerological meaning. If a trump card repeats a number shown by multiple pip cards—for example three Threes and the Empress—the creative and amalgamating influence of the number three has an emphasized impact on the period. A predominance of court cards indicates social and interpersonal activities, with Kings and Queens indicative of one-on-one conversations and Knights and Pages representing group events.

A high number of trump cards indicates that several important events will bring notable consequences that last beyond the forecast period. Each trump card that appears in a week-trio should be considered to determine if its influence is friendly or adverse. It should also be closely compared to the other cards in its trio to determine the area of life most likely to be affected.

Summing Up

Although the Forecast Spread might seem rather complex, it has great advantages for beginning tarotists. As each seven-day period is completed, the tarotist can review the relevance of that week's card trio and gain understanding of the mundane implications of card combinations through hindsight. Compare the events of each week to the cards that appeared for that week, and note any additional mundane interpretations that could be connected with those cards. These observations can form the basis of a personal seventy-eight–card notebook, where new and expanded interpretations of the cards can be gathered.

Where the weekly trios can be reviewed for mundane interpretations, information can also be gathered regarding the implications of the central card. Many spreads contains a "querent" card, and this is often (erroneously) considered as a static representation. The tarotist can consider the ways in which the central card has symbolized his or her inner evolution and outer roles during the forecast period. As the period ends, review the entire spread to evaluate how the central card has shifted from the beginning to the end of the four weeks. A thorough retrospective review will show the wide range of meanings that the central card can encompass from an inner, meditative standpoint.

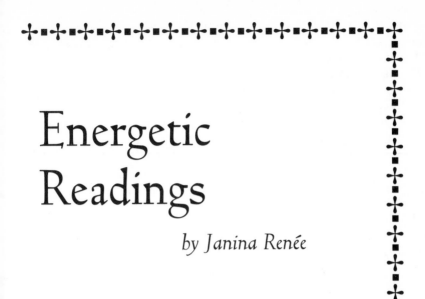

Energetic Readings

by Janina Renée

Many Americans complain about not having enough energy. In fact, low energy is something of an epidemic. And although we usually think of energy loss as an older folks' concern, it is just as likely to be a problem for young people, including school children. Perhaps we can blame this on the conditions of modern life, which promote bad habits, put our sleep-wake cycles out of sync with nature, discourage a healthy balance of work and play, and keep piling on complications. This is a serious issue, because this energy shortage can adversely affect all areas of a person's life. For example, because personal energy levels determine individuals' ability to succeed, they often make the difference between the "haves" and the "have-nots."

A person's energy level is also something that may be discerned among the other conditions portrayed in a tarot reading, and it is a good indicator as to whether your subject will be able to manifest whatever potentially favorable outcomes may be indicated in the cards. When I get a reading that shows both favorable and unfavorable influences at work, I put extra weight on the energy factor.

Because they can pertain to the quality of a person's energy, the appearance of the Strength card, Temperance, the Sun, the Magician, the Ace of Wands, and the Ace of Swords are all indicators that your subject has a good chance of fulfilling his or her goals. On the other hand, the reversal of these cards puts a desirable outcome in greater doubt. Depending on the position of the cards in a reading, it may be that the person may initially make progress but then lose steam, or perhaps there is a problem with his or her energy coming sporadically, in fits, stops, and starts. Nevertheless, the fact that these cards have come up at all suggests that the potential for the needed energy is there, as long as your subject is willing to pay more attention to bodily health, and ready to nurture enthusiasm.

In their upright positions, the court cards or other cards that are acting as a person's significator show your querent to be strong in his or her power, which also suggests a good quality of personal energy and the likelihood of success. Reversed significator cards can indicate a lot of different things, but energy problems can certainly be implicated. Indeed, energy deficiencies can be implicated in any reversed card—even the Devil, as in some cases this card pertains to libidinal energy, and this is something that all of us need in order to maintain our lust for life.

To achieve an optimum energy flow, a person needs to work at bringing his or her life into just the right balance, the right combination of influences. This theme is a major preoccupation of the tarot as a whole, and may be repeated throughout a course of readings. Cards including Temperance, Justice, the Star, the World, and all of the Twos (and various other cards that portray twins, opposites, or mirrored images) can speak to this need. Their reversals may warn that more adjustment is needed. The conditions that require modulation may be indicated by the cards that flank them: Swords, Wands, and odd-numbered cards may point to activities; Cups, Pentacles, and even-numbered cards may denote concerns about stability or rest. Other clues may be taken from the elemental associations, such as whether or not the qualities of fire, earth, air, or water are well balanced or harmonious.

If energy requirements are a concern, you can address a reading to this issue, asking the tarot something like, "What can you tell me about my energy level?" or "Why don't I have enough pep?"

Here is an example of a reading in response to such a question. Using a version of the *Rider-Waite-Smith* deck, a certain woman drew the Seven of Wands, the reversed Seven of Pentacles, and the Seven of Swords. From the central card, we can see that disappointed and delayed expectations are at the core of the problem. This has an obvious application to the querent's life situation, as she is a small-business person, and, despite her hard work, her success has been slow in taking off. Also, note the interesting occurrence of all Sevens: seven is characteristically a number for individualistic and innovative people who are going it alone while facing outside pressures, competition, and other challenges to their ideas and lifestyles. Such challenges are certainly draining.

To learn how you can boost your energy, you can also go to the tarot for an advice reading, asking, "What do I need to do to get more energy?"

In such a follow-up question to the previous reading example, the business woman got the Seven of Pentacles reversed, the World reversed, and the Three of Cups. Briefly put, this reading suggests a need to limit her spheres of activity and to learn to live with slow growth and reduced expectations—at least for the time being. Notice how the same card, the reversed Seven of Pentacles, appeared as a card denoting the situation in the previous reading and as a suggested course of action in the advice reading. This indicates that she's generally been doing the right things, and the course of her life is going about as well as can be expected. The party-going Three of Cups may seem to contradict the other cards' advice, but in this context it may recommend not worrying so much, and biding her time with casual, noncommittal enjoyment of good times with friends and community as a way to regain her vitality. (By "noncommittal" I mean that she should avoid organizing or volunteering for anything; she should just go along for the fun.)

The other way that the tarot can help you with energy issues is by providing archetypes that you can model—though of course different people will want to work with different images, depending on how their energy needs to be modulated. Thus, the previously mentioned business-woman might do well to find satisfaction in the process (rather than the product) of her work by identifying with an easygoing version of the Knight or Queen of Pentacles. For people who need to get more done, the Wands court cards make good role models, though some may have to resist the impulse to take on too many projects. Because I come from a family that discouraged initiative, I am sometimes slow to take necessary action, so when I recognize this inertia I propel myself forward by visualizing the Knight of Wands, and even humming a little jingle that goes, "That's what the active person does!" Of course, for getting all of your energies pulled together, Major Arcana cards like the Magician, Strength, Temperance, the Star, and the World are especially inspiring.

Reading for Children: 12 Tips

by Corrine Kenner

My daughter Julia has a deck of tarot cards. She looks through it when we're watching television in the living room. She pulls cards for her sisters, and they study the images together. Sometimes she even takes the deck to play with at her grandmother's house.

Unfortunately, some of the cards are missing, and some of them are bent. But that's understandable—Julia is only a year old.

Granted, she's a little young for the complexities of the tarot. Before long, however, I fully expect that she'll want me to give her "real" tarot readings—almost as often as she'll want me to read to her from her favorite volume of Dr. Seuss.

While the tarot is usually used to examine the questions and concerns of adults, it's an equally effective tool for young people. Children have issues that are as serious to them as the problems faced by their elders. The desire to please parents, teachers, and coaches can make some youngsters as anxious as career-minded adults working for a promotion. Homework, tests, and pop quizzes are a constant source of stress. Add sibling rivalry, peer pressure, and adolescent hormones to the mix, and it's no surprise that some kids are practically nervous wrecks. It could even be argued that young people need a tool like the tarot even more than adults, because they typically haven't developed the resources and coping mechanisms that maturity brings.

In fact, it can be extremely rewarding to read tarot cards for children. Young people are often more enthusiastic about tarot readings than adults. They're happy to talk about themselves, open in their descriptions of their questions and concerns, and eager to get advice from a seemingly neutral third party like the tarot. What's more, children are usually unreserved in their comments or criticisms of the images on each card, and willing to give you valuable feedback about your accuracy as a reader.

Children's readings do vary from the sessions that are typically conducted for adults. However, with a few simple changes in technique, it's possible to give rich and rewarding tarot card readings to clients of any age. Here are some tips to keep in mind.

1. Choose a G-rated deck. Selecting a deck for children's readings is very much like choosing a deck for public readings at psychic fairs and festivals. The decks should be eye-catching, colorful, and suitable for all audiences. They shouldn't depict naked people, or gruesome bloody Swords, or shocking, violent images like the Grim Reaper mowing down a series of hapless victims.

The standard *Universal Tarot*, *Rider-Waite-Smith*, *Voyager Tarot*, *Whimsical Tarot*, the *Tarot of Oz*, and *Alice in Wonderland* decks are all good choices for children's readings.

In fact, if you are reading for very young or school-age children, you may wish to eliminate frightening or disturbing images altogether. It's probably best to pull the Death card, the Devil, and the Ten of Swords out of the deck before you shuffle and spread the cards. There will still be enough cards left to give an accurate, effective reading.

2. Get the parents' permission. When children ask you for a tarot reading, check with their parents before you begin. Ask, "Is it okay with you if we look at these cards together?" You might want to reassure them that your readings will be lighthearted by adding, "It's just for fun."

If parents say "no," be gracious and support their decision. It doesn't mean they're bigoted or overprotective. It's possible that they're simply in a hurry—or that they've never had a reading themselves, and that they're unwilling to experience their first reading with their children involved.

If parents aren't available—for example, if you are reading in public or a child is visiting your home—don't take chances. Even if you're fairly certain that a reading would be okay with a parent, you might want to limit the reading to a single card, and keep it light and upbeat. If a child draws an Ace of Wands, for example, your reading can be as simple as saying, "You are a talented, creative person. You could be a writer or an artist!"

3. Explain the process. Before each reading begins, explain how you plan to shuffle, spread, and read the cards. You might even need to explain what tarot cards are. Keep your descriptions simple. Tarot cards are commonly known as fortunetelling cards. Even if you personally use them in more complex ways, you can certainly introduce them that way to a child. Alternatively, you can tell your young clients that tarot cards can be used to tell stories about their lives, and that they can suggest solutions to their problems.

4. Keep your readings age-appropriate. You can read cards for curious children as young as three or four. Of course, your reading style—your vocabulary, your explanations, and your attitude—will vary according to the age of your client.

You may want to relate the images on each card to stories, movies, and television shows that youngsters will recognize. You could compare the Fool, for example, to Pinocchio, or the Emperor to Captain Kirk.

Your intention is also an important factor in a child's reading. As you prepare yourself to read for a youngster, plan to focus only on the positive so that you can offer an uplifting and optimistic reading.

5. Clarify each child's questions or concerns. When you read tarot cards for an adult, it's helpful for you to know which areas your client wants to explore. The same holds true for your readings with children.

Until most kids are seven or eight, however, they won't know how to articulate a question for the cards. They can tell you what they like to do—which games they like to play, for instance—which could give you some direction. For the most part, however, you'll probably have the best results if your readings simply focus on each child's talents and abilities. Use the cards to pinpoint their strengths, praise their accomplishments, and to encourage them in their development.

Children in elementary school are some of the most appealing clients, because they are able to pinpoint their questions and concerns—and they're unfailingly honest about their questions and concerns. You can get by with asking an opening question that gets right to the point, such as, "Do you have any questions about the future?" or, "Do you have any problems?"

Teenagers are not always so open. They typically want to keep their issues private. You may want to offer a generalized suggestion for the reading, such as friends, family issues, relationships, or school, which you can both use as a starting point.

6. Keep your readings short. Most preschoolers have an attention span of about thirty seconds, so your readings should take about fifteen seconds. One or two sentences highlighting a preschooler's talents, abilities, and potential is more than sufficient.

A reading for a child in elementary school should last five or ten minutes, and a reading for a teenager should generally run from fifteen to twenty minutes.

If you normally charge money for tarot readings, consider charging little or nothing for children's readings. Preschoolers' readings should be free, because they should be extremely brief and essentially painless. So, in most cases, should readings for elementary school children. Think of them as a goodwill gesture toward their parents, who may become paying customers. You might want to offer a deep discount rate for teenagers—but to encourage their investment in the reading process, ask that they pay for it themselves, without help from their parents.

7. Make sure that children are active participants, not simply observers. Children and teenagers will connect with the cards and get more from a reading if they are actively involved in the process of reading.

Start the traditional way, by shuffling the deck. While most youngsters can't shuffle an oversized tarot deck themselves, they can cut the cards, and that's enough to imbue the deck with their energy and intention.

Before you let them touch your cards, however, you might want to check their hands. Kids can be kind of sticky. You might want to ask them to wash up before you begin, or keep a package of wet wipes handy.

Once you've laid the cards are on the table, actively draw each child into the reading. Ask questions that will help them picture themselves in the spread, like, "Which card looks like you?" or, "How does this card remind you of your situation?" You could even ask, "What does this picture mean to you?"

8. Involve the parents. When you read tarot cards for young people, you may find yourself dealing with ethical considerations and responsibilities that don't come up when you read for adults. All of your clients, regardless of age, deserve the same degree of compassion and respect. Unlike adults, however, young people don't need—or expect—the same level of privacy that adults require.

In fact, it's probably a good idea to have a parent present during a child's tarot reading. Parents need to know what information their children are getting from other adults, and you need to protect yourself against misunderstandings.

It's a simple fact that the actual amount of privacy that each individual needs varies by age. I've developed what I call the "bathtub rule" to use as a guideline. If children are still young enough to need a parent to watch them while they're in the tub, they should have a parent present at their tarot reading too. Elementary school children can usually bathe themselves, but they often need help rinsing the

shampoo out of their hair; their parents should be on hand for a tarot reading, as well. And while teenagers will typically lock and barricade a bathroom door to protect their privacy, their parents still pay for the hot water they use. Teenagers' parents have a right to know—at least in general terms—what their kids are up to.

The actual amount of parental participation in a tarot reading should also vary by age. Very young children should be sitting on a parents' lap—in part so that parents can keep their youngsters from pulling all of the cards off the table, but also to offer feedback and help you interpret the cards in language that their children will understand.

Elementary school children may sit next to a parent, but those parents should be silent observers. You should encourage school-age children to ask their own questions, and you should discuss the cards directly with them.

And the parents of teenagers should probably linger somewhere in the background, within earshot but with that far-away expression parents of teens learn to adopt when they're in public together.

Most of your readings for young people will involve fairly predictable issues: concerns about parents, siblings, school, and playmates. If by some odd chance, however, a young person confides in you that they are in harm's way—from drugs, alcohol, or the like—end the reading. Rather than offering the child your advice, tell the parents about the problem.

9. Offer specific advice and suggestions that children can use. Children typically don't understand long-winded explanations about archetypes, synchronicity, or the collective unconscious. They need specific advice that relates directly to their own lives, and concrete suggestions for actions that they can initiate. They also appreciate being placed in a position of power and control over their own lives.

For every card that you read for a child or a teenager, find a clear and succinct message that will make sense, or a suggestion that they can follow. If a young person draws the Hanged Man, for example, recommend a solitary activity like journaling.

And remember, just as with adults, you might be the only tarot reader that some children ever see; the messages you relay during a reading may stay with them for the rest of their lives. Avoid making any predictions that could become a self-fulfilling prophecy or limit a child's growth in any way.

10. Make sure each child understands the reading. As you conclude, ask your young clients to repeat what they've heard or
describe what they've learned. Then clarify the cards' message if
necessary.

11. Set limits. Children, just like some adults, thrive on the one-on-
one attention they receive during a tarot reading. Some may linger
at the table and never want to leave. You might want to make a
habit of telling your young clients, before you begin, how long you
will spend with them. "I will read three cards: one for your past,
one for your present, and one for your future." When you're
through, say, "We'll have to wrap this up now. I can only answer
one more question."

12. Send them away happy. It's easiest to conclude a children's
reading by sending them off with a parting gift. You might want to
end each reading by letting children draw a single card from an
extra, give-away tarot deck. You could also write a one-sentence
summary of their reading on a colorful piece of note paper or the
back of your business card. You could even give them a small pol-
ished stone or a lucky penny to keep as a token of their reading.

No matter how you conduct a tarot reading for a child, you'll
probably find that you enjoy it as much—if not more—than reading for adults, and that it's possible to remain true to the nature and
the meanings of the cards regardless of your clients' age.

A Closer Look At:

Legend: The Arthurian Tarot

Created and illustrated by
Anna-Marie Ferguson

- 78 full-color cards and a 276-page illustrated book

- Cards are 4¾ x 2¾, with nonreversible backs and illustrated pips

- Beautiful watercolor paintings synthesize *Rider-Waite-Smith* imagery with medieval art traditions to illustrate characters and stories from Arthurian legend

- Deck symbolism draws upon Celtic legend, historical references, medieval romances, and Grail Quest myths

- Illustrated companion book is a primer for Arthurian legend, explaining the story behind each character and event in the deck

Tarot and Astrology

by Christine Jette

B ecause I am a Libra Sun, with Libra rising and a Cancer Moon, I can't think about two things without trying to establish a relationship between them on a deeper level. I believe the blending of tarot and astrology is meant to be useful. By understanding and applying what we learn, we know ourselves better and improve our lives because of it.

The Happy Birthday layout that follows can be used with any Sun sign. This simplified layout, blending tarot and astrology, offers you speed and ease—and yields a lot of detailed, personal information despite its simplicity. You do not need to be a lifelong student of either discipline to work with it, but I offer a cautionary word about simplicity: tarot readers and astrologers acquire their skills over time, and nothing compares to an in-depth reading or natal report. This spread, however, will get you started, so enjoy getting to know the one-and-only you.

Happy Birthday Layout

Rarely does the tarot give specific instructions, such as "Move to Rhode Island and open a metaphysical shop." But the tarot does offer a sense of what we need, the right direction to go for our greatest good. This layout can be used any time you want to align

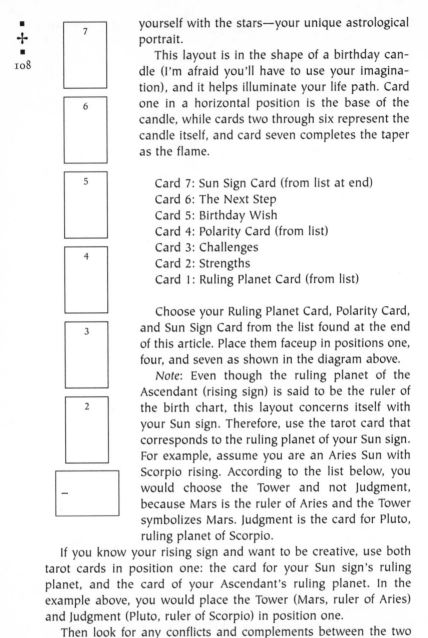

yourself with the stars—your unique astrological portrait.

This layout is in the shape of a birthday candle (I'm afraid you'll have to use your imagination), and it helps illuminate your life path. Card one in a horizontal position is the base of the candle, while cards two through six represent the candle itself, and card seven completes the taper as the flame.

Card 7: Sun Sign Card (from list at end)
Card 6: The Next Step
Card 5: Birthday Wish
Card 4: Polarity Card (from list)
Card 3: Challenges
Card 2: Strengths
Card 1: Ruling Planet Card (from list)

Choose your Ruling Planet Card, Polarity Card, and Sun Sign Card from the list found at the end of this article. Place them faceup in positions one, four, and seven as shown in the diagram above.

Note: Even though the ruling planet of the Ascendant (rising sign) is said to be the ruler of the birth chart, this layout concerns itself with your Sun sign. Therefore, use the tarot card that corresponds to the ruling planet of your Sun sign. For example, assume you are an Aries Sun with Scorpio rising. According to the list below, you would choose the Tower and not Judgment, because Mars is the ruler of Aries and the Tower symbolizes Mars. Judgment is the card for Pluto, ruling planet of Scorpio.

If you know your rising sign and want to be creative, use both tarot cards in position one: the card for your Sun sign's ruling planet, and the card of your Ascendant's ruling planet. In the example above, you would place the Tower (Mars, ruler of Aries) and Judgment (Pluto, ruler of Scorpio) in position one.

Then look for any conflicts and complements between the two cards as you do the layout. For instance, how does the Tower interact with Judgment? What is the conflict or complement of energy?

Don't old forms have to fall (the Tower) before the karmic slate can be cleared (Judgment)? I am convinced that it is the relationship of one card to another in a layout that yields the most useful information, but then, I view the universe through the lens of relationships.

Shuffle the remaining cards, concentrating on any concerns that you now want answered. (If it is actually your birthday, be sure to make a wish!) When you are ready, randomly select four cards, facedown, and place them in positions two, three, five, and six, as shown in the diagram above. Turn the four cards over and read the layout as follows.

Position 1: My Ruling Planet Card

The driving energy of the layout. All other cards are read in relationship to it.

If you like the card, it means you are comfortable with its energy and know how to use it for growth. If you do not like the card, it indicates an area that needs your attention because it is the dominant energy around you. Best to make friends with it, or at least be attuned to the lessons it has to offer you.

Position 2: My Strengths

Where you shine, your talents and abilities. Where the energy flows without resistance. What to keep and nurture because it makes you strong.

If you like the card, you are using its energy to its highest potential. If the card makes you uncomfortable, it indicates an area that is blocked and needs work. If you work with the message of this card, it will release its energy and make you strong. Now ask yourself, how does Card 2 (Strengths) relate to your Ruling Planet Card, the driving energy of the layout? Note any conflicts and complements.

Position 3: My Challenges

Your life lessons or energy blocks. What you need to face in order to grow. Areas where you get stuck and may keep repeating the same patterns.

If you like this card, try reading it in its reversed or shadow form. Maybe you are getting too much of a good thing? For example, what if the Sun comes up here? What could be wrong with that? Well, plenty, if its golden rays are giving you sunburn or burnout. Being comfortable with this card can also mean you are facing your challenges head-on and doing the work you need to do. If you don't like the card, it indicates an area (block) where you know you need to work to release its energy for growth. Now ask yourself, how does Card 3 (Challenges) relate to your Ruling Planet Card, the driving energy of the layout? Note any conflicts and complements.

Position 4: My Polarity Card, The Sister Sign

The opposite of you, showing your dual nature. What you need to draw toward you and attract in order to feel complete.

Polarity, your opposite sign, is your "sister sign" because the energy is like your own Sun sign in a complementary way. This is the duality, or balance, of you. The card may make you uncomfortable because it feels foreign to you. It may even feel like your "evil twin," but rest assured, this card is you—the other half of you. If you like the card, you are incorporating its energy into your life. The question to ask yourself is: what do you need to learn and incorporate into your life to achieve balance? Now ask yourself, how does Card 4 (Polarity) relate to your Ruling Planet Card, the driving energy of the layout? Note any conflicts and complements.

Position 5: What is my birthday wish?

This card gives focus to your deepest desires and hopes, the true direction of your life path, because your dreams and desires come from your higher self, which is a sacred part of you.

If you like this card, it means you are on the right track for the fullest expression of your Sun sign. If the card makes you uncomfortable, it indicates the energy that is standing in your way. You will have to deal with its energy (the block) before your sacred dreams can become reality. Now ask yourself, how does Card 5 (Birthday Wish) relate to your Ruling Planet Card, the driving energy of the layout? Note any conflicts and complements.

Position 6: The Next Step (The Future)

Where do you go from here? What is the next step on your life path for the fullest expression of your Sun sign personality?

If you like this card, be glad and look forward to the next adventure. If this card makes you uncomfortable, it indicates a possible upcoming life lesson. While the life lesson may be no fun, it will offer you wisdom and make you strong.

Remember, the cards, like astrology, *impel* rather than *compel*. *Nothing in tarot is preordained*. The cards either describe a situation or give advice about a situation. If you don't like this card, work with the energy of the other cards to see how you can change its direction. You always have the power of choice to change what is no longer useful and create your own future—or at least face the future with courage. Now ask yourself, how does Card 6 (The Next Step/Future) relate to your Ruling Planet Card, the driving energy of the layout? Note any conflicts and complements.

Position 7: My Sun Sign Card, The Essence of Me

What you were put here to learn, the focal point of this lifetime.

The Sun sign card is in the flame of the candle because it shows your true nature and represents your spirit. It remains constant throughout the year. It illuminates your conscious purpose, your drive to achieve goals, and the "You" you know yourself to be.

Bottom line: do you like this card? How comfortable are you with yourself? How does Card 7 (Sun Sign) relate to your Ruling Planet Card, the driving energy of the layout? Note any conflicts and complements. Especially note conflicts and complements if you have chosen to use the Ruling Planet Card for your rising sign (Ascendant), in position one. The ruling planet of your rising sign is the true driving energy of your birth chart.

Putting It All Together

Look at cards one, four, and seven. Do you see relationships or conflicts between the driving energy of your layout (Ruling Planet Card), your sister sign (Polarity Card), and the essence of you (the Sun Sign Card)? How can you use cards two (Strengths), three (Challenges), five (Wishes), and six (The Next Step), to align yourself with the essence of your Sun sign personality for its fullest expression?

It may help to make an entry in your tarot journal. You can also leave the cards out for a while, or program a dream, for more insight. It may help to use your favorite three-card spread for more information on any card in the layout. For added depth, you can read a description of your ruling planet, polarity sign, and Sun sign in a basic astrology book. The relationships of

the specific tarot card meanings and their corresponding signs and planets are amazingly similar.

Your astrological cards have special significance when they appear in any layout. Not only did your unconscious mind bring the card to your reading, but the heavens are communicating with you too. Blending tarot with astrology yields fresh insight into the significance of each card for you, and gives a fresh perspective on your personality by way of the zodiac. Pay attention, because the stars are trying to talk to you.

The Happy Birthday layout can be easily incorporated into your professional tarot service. One idea is to offer gift certificates that your clients can give to friends or family as unique birthday presents. You can advertise it as the perfect gift for the person who has everything, or for the person who is difficult to please. Place an expiration date on the certificate—three months from the gift recipient's birth date, or client's date of purchase, is reasonable.

If you use my layout in your professional practice, (and I hope you do), I ask only that you tell others who created it and where you found it. Thank you. Now make a wish for the coming year and may all your dreams come true.

Happy birthday!

Tarot Card Correspondences

Dates of Sun signs vary slightly. You may also have been born on the cusp of a sign, which means your birthday falls on the transition day between one sign and the next. If so, you can determine your true Sun sign with a simple computerized birth chart, using the date, location, and exact time of your birth.

ARIES (March 21 - April 19)
Ruling Planet: Mars (The Tower)
Polarity: Libra (Justice)
Sun Sign Card (The Emperor)

TAURUS (April 20 - May 20)
Ruling Planet: Venus (The Empress)
Polarity: Scorpio (Death)
Sun Sign Card (The Hierophant)

GEMINI (May 21 - June 20)
Ruling Planet: Mercury (The Magician)
Polarity: Sagittarius (Temperance)
Sun Sign Card (The Lovers)

CANCER (June 21 - July 22)
Ruling Planet: Moon (The High Priestess)
Polarity: Capricorn (The Devil)
Sun Sign Card (The Chariot)

LEO (July 23 - August 22)
Ruling Planet: Sun (The Sun)
Polarity: Aquarius (Star)
Sun Sign Card (Strength)

VIRGO (August 23 - September 22)
Ruling Planet: Mercury (The Magician)
Polarity: Pisces (The Moon)
Sun Sign Card (The Hermit)

Tarot Card Correspondences

LIBRA (September 23 - October 22)
Ruling Planet: Venus (The Empress)
Polarity: Aries (The Emperor)
Sun Sign Card (Justice)

SCORPIO (October 23 - November 21)
Ruling Planet: Pluto (Judgment)
Polarity: Taurus (Hierophant)
Sun Sign Card (Death)

SAGITTARIUS (November 22 - December 21)
Ruling Planet: Jupiter (Wheel of Fortune)
Polarity: Gemini (The Lovers)
Sun Sign Card (Temperance)

CAPRICORN (December 22 - January 19)
Ruling Planet: Saturn (The World)
Polarity: Cancer (The Chariot)
Sun Sign Card (The Devil)

AQUARIUS (January 20 - February 18)
Ruling Planet: Uranus (The Fool)
Polarity: Leo (Strength)
Sun Sign Card (The Star)

PISCES (February 19 - March 20)
Ruling Planet: Neptune (Hanged Man)
Polarity: Virgo (The Hermit)
Sun Sign Card (The Moon)

The Meta Celtic Cross

by Kevin Quigley

E ven the most straightforward reading using the Celtic Cross spread is one based on relationships. The reader must combine a card meaning with the meaning of its respective position. For years this is how I used the spread: ten cards, ten positions, and ten interpretations combined into one single message. But as my own spiritual awareness grew, I began to see life as a constantly shifting system of patterns or fields. All my experience seemed to fit into a larger pattern with no distinct borders, a sort of web—a change in any one part affecting all others. This, to me, is a beautiful synchronicity.

I began to search for patterns in the cards when doing a spread. Two Knights might appear in a single reading, or three related trumps, perhaps a few reversed Wands. I'd look more intuitively at those cards and their positions. What were they trying to tell me? Eventually, this style of reading began to supplant the card-by-card approach and my applications of the cross expanded dramatically. As my exploration into the use of patterns continued, a number of them seemed to emerge from within the layout of the cross itself. I think of these as meta-positions presiding over and above—and interacting with—the individual card positions. And I call this approach meta-reading.

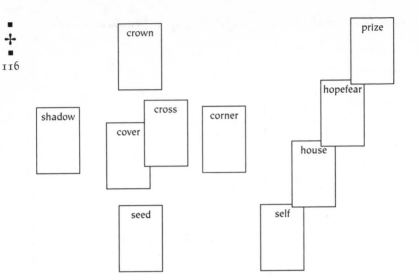

Let us begin with a broad look at the Celtic Cross. We have ten cards that immediately divide into two major groups: the six cards on the left arranged into a large three-by-three cross, and a stack of four on the right. Employing a basic symbolic interpretation of "left" and "right"—that of material objectivity and energetic subjectivity respectively—allows us to attach meaning to each set. The cross-and-ring grouping on the left is the objective group representing a moment as it really is. These are the "situational" cards. The stack on the right represents feelings, emotions, attitudes, and energy, as opposed to actual facts. These are the "motivational" cards.

Next, we can break the situational set down into two perspectives, each of which uses all of the cards. The first I call *nowHere*. Pronounced as "now-here," it is a reminder to focus our attention on the present, for it is only the moment before us that offers any true possibility of growth. When voiced as "no-where," we paint an ephemeral picture of the cosmos. What is past resides in the mind as memory. What could be is at best merely speculation. They are both products of the mind. All we have is this moment, right now, and it too will fade. At the fundamental core, where we are is both now-here and nowhere, and they are one in the same.

I have named the second perspective *coagula-solve*. It comes from an alchemical term meaning to "coagulate and dissolve" and illustrates the cyclical creative process that is the cosmos. From this perspective, the physical world is really a manifestation of divine energy. Underneath all the objectivity of things is a pulsating universe of light. I believe Einstein's famous equation, $E = mc^2$, can be viewed as a poem describing this very idea. Energy is matter and matter, energy. And each and every moment we experience is the result of the beautiful dance shared by these two partners.

So, we have two complementary ways of approaching the situational set: one focusing on the constantly changing instant of time we call *nowHere* and the other on the interconnected process of an unfolding universe forever condensing into matter and dissolving into light. But how do we make practical use of these perspectives? We do so by recognizing that they themselves are also dyads, by breaking them one final time into their own pairs of yin-yang components. It is the resulting four groups that we employ while doing a reading.

The *nowHere* dyad is composed of the two cards crossed in the center as balanced by the four surrounding cards. I refer to the crossed pair as the "central" cards and the other four as the "circumstantial" cards. Remember, we are still in the situational set of the spread, so all of our interpretations will revolve around the actual facts of the situation. The central cards represent the situation itself, where we are and what we find immediately before us, quite literally the crossroads at which we currently stand. These cards operate as a team. How do they comment on one another? How does the crossing card challenge or color the crossed? Do they approach each other with a sense of harmony or is there discord in their juxtaposition? This is the now-here function as it concerns what is right before us.

To examine the nowhere aspect of the dyad, look at the four circumstantial cards (*circum* = circle). These cards give us a sense of the conditions and/or events surrounding the current situation. Is it a supportive environment or is there a lot of strife in the "neighborhood?" Is the conversation between these four cards clear and concise or is it full of confusion and mixed messages? This is a great way to make use of a spread whose cards just don't seem to gel. When one looks at a spread only to find a miasma of cards that just won't seem to mesh, it can help to divide the spread into these groups to see if the confusing elements are isolated into a single set, and incorporate that information into an interpretation. For example, in this type of situation one will often find that the central cards lend themselves to a clear description, but the periphery is confusing. What might this sort of situational "eye-of-the-hurricane" have to say about the goings on, or how to proceed? Should these conditions be reversed, the central cross making little sense and the circumstances appearing clearly, then perhaps we hear a call to simply raise one's head and take a look at what is going on around us.

It is important to sum up the relationship between these two sets. Recapitulate your interpretations of the center and the circumstance, then take a moment to look into how they might interrelate. For example, if the central situation addresses a need to persevere through a difficult time and the circumstances talk about feelings of defeat and giving up one might conclude that the environment itself has created this sense of burden. The only way out may be through.

For the second dyad, *coagula-solve*, we divide the situational set into the three horizontal versus the three vertical cards. The horizontal axis depicts the plane of the earth, the material realm, space-time. The left card represents where we are coming from, the center where we are now, and the right where we are headed. Rather than view these as three distinct entities (past, present, and future), it is more helpful to see them as a blended moment. Here we have a past that has unfolded naturally into the present moment we are experiencing. This moment, given how we got here and who we are, has already set up its inevitable undoing. This is not the theoretical future of some great distance that we may affect by expanding our consciousness (something we are doing at this very moment by reading tarot), which is both very real and very valid. This is the next moment, so related to the now that we will

experience it in the same sense that we draw a new breath after finishing each exhalation. This is how we read the "physical" subset. How do the cards reflect upon each other as if in a continuum? Is it clear that where we just were has prepared us for where we are, and where we are is preparing us for what is next? If not, can you describe the gap? When a disjunction appears between two cards in this subset, when the question of "How did I get here from there?" arises, it is helpful to look at how the cards *don't* fit to see how they might. This is similar to building a puzzle: once we have enough pieces to make the shape of the missing one clear, finding it is simply a matter of looking.

The second subset is treated in very similar fashion to the first. However, where the physical subset deals with actual events in our lives, the second deals with the spiritual. The bottom card represents the "seed" of the current situation, one of the greater lessons we have been dealing with for a long time. Looking back through the path of one's life, one inevitably finds that the difficulties with which we have been presented often have a common theme or pattern. Life presents us with the same situation over and over again (usually at increasing levels of intensity) until we learn how to handle it, and then we move on to the next. This seed card points to the "lesson" that has devised the situation we are now experiencing. It tells us to remember these times, to assess the choices we made that worked and those that didn't. An honest appraisal of how we acted then might help us to make better choices now. The center card, the first card we lay, represents our current spiritual state. Making the connection between this state and the lesson represented below is paramount to understanding this moment in its greater spiritual context. How can this moment be seen as an opportunity to make progress within the larger lesson? Above us is the "crown." This card calls forth a message from our greater self. The greater self is the source of dreams and nightmares, it is the source of inspiration, it is the great ocean from which we draw the new aspects of who we are as our lives expand and grow.

These two groups together, the physical and the spiritual, illustrate the fundamental process through which the divine energy is manifest in the world around us. The vertical path from top to bottom represents the drawing down of this energy into the lower, material world: coagulation. We can see this illustrated in the card of the Magician, the hand on the left side of the card raises a wand to the heavens, the instrument of drawing forth this energy, while the hand on the right points to the earth, directing the energy downward. The horizontal represents a physical world rife with divine energy, and as we grow from past to future this can be understood as an advancement to a higher energetic state: dissolution.

We have dissected the six situational cards into four subsets. The first pair of subsets, known together as *nowHere*, deals with our current situation and set of circumstances. The second, *coagula-solve*, expresses how the physical and spiritual/energetic realms cooperate to produce the moments we experience. It is possible to compare the ways in which these two aspects comment on each other. One is a look at a single moment by the events and relationships which reflect it in any number of ways The other is a realization of life as a continuum of such moments that bleed into each other as watercolor on an oversaturated piece of paper.

Moving on, the second major set within the Celtic Cross, the motivational stack on the right, often receives short shrift in interpretation. We get so tied up in our lives that we forget to recognize how we feel about it all. This is a grave error, literally, for when one reassembles the cards of this spread into an actual Celtic Cross (employed often as a headstone), the four cards on the right form the stem beneath the cross and the ring. Our situation does not influence how we feel—but how we feel, in fact, creates our situation! Each of these four cards is directly related to one of the four subsets of the six situational cards of the cross and ring. These relationships form the web of influence between our inner lives and our outer experience. When viewed this way, one could consider this stack as an extension of the spiritual vertical axis, part of the *coagula-solve* with a direct connection to the divine energy. This is why I refer to this set as "motivational," where the real action happens.

The bottom card in the stack represents the *self*. It describes our attitude, how we are feeling with regard to the situation at hand. This card relates to the two central cards of the cross. When we combine this card with what we already know of the center of our situation, great insights can be learned. Rather than viewing this card as a reaction to the situation, invert the relationship and see how this frame of mind may have contributed to bringing the current opportunity about. This is very much a relationship of "You reap what you sow." As the bottom card in the stack, it is the foundation of the entire cross above. Attitude is everything.

Above the card of self, we have the card of *house*. This deals with the energy we draw to us (the attitudes of those close to us, and those who may have something at stake in the situation). It is how we are perceived, or how we think we are being perceived, and how this might affect our actions. It is responsible for the circumstantial cards of the ring. A simple illustration of the idea is that the friends we choose have an effect on our life. Do we hang with a more cynical crowd, ready to disbelieve or tear something down? Or are our friends more optimistic and supportive? We can all find moments in our lives when we failed to live up to our higher potential, and may discover that those choices were reflected in the quality of our social group.

The cards in the motivational stack represent our real choices. It is our choice of emotions that determine more of our path in life than any random external event. Anyone can have his wallet stolen, but do you choose to rant and rave at the injustice or do you laugh at your foolishness of leaving it unattended the counter? These cards are about recognizing our feelings about the moment we are experiencing, so as not to slip into the habit of allowing our lesser qualities to make all the decisions.

The third card, what I refer to as *hopefear* (one word) calls to our attention what may be the primary motivating factor in how we make our decisions: we reach for what we hope to gain and run from what we fear to encounter. How often have we made a hasty decision based on these emotions only to regret it later? This card calls our attention to a strong emotion that may have an unconscious influence on our actions, and asks us to stop and consider for a moment: "Is this really what I want to be doing?"

Hopefear is related to the horizontal, physical axis of the situational cards. It is real-world decisions we are making, and it is to the real world that we must look for their impact. How does the picture of where we were, are, and will be interact with our *hopefear* as indicated by this card? Face your fears and do not be owned by your hopes.

The final card in the spread I call the *prize*. It stands just beneath cross and ring, taking all of its weight. If the base position of *self* is the foundation, then this is the structural point upon which the cross holds together. Commonly called "outcome," to me, it represents something more. This card represents the goal of the soul, why we are here leading this life, encountering these situations. As the seed card infers, we experience the same lessons time and again until we overcome whatever illusions we cling to and accept the world as it really is, and grow. It is this growth that is represented by the *prize*. It is the new insight our greater self has grasped. It is the only gift our small, ego-bound selves can give to the greater aspect of ourselves. The gift we get in return is some small understanding of truth and the sense of being more solid, wiser, more real, and closer to the most beautiful version of ourselves we could possibly imagine.

The Wheel

2005 Almanac

26 Sunday

Moon in Cancer
Full Moon 10:06 am

Kwanzaa begins

27 Monday

Moon in Cancer

28 Tuesday

Moon in Cancer
Moon enters Leo 12:14 pm

29 Wednesday

Moon in Leo

30 Thursday

Moon in Leo

31 Friday

Moon in Leo
Moon enters Virgo 12:33 am

New Year's Eve

1 Saturday

Moon in Virgo

New Year's Day ♦ Kwanzaa ends

2 Sunday

Moon in Virgo
Moon enters Libra 11:19 am

3 Monday

Moon in Libra
Fourth Quarter 12:46 pm

4 Tuesday

Moon in Libra
Moon enters Scorpio 7:00 pm

5 Wednesday

Moon in Scorpio

6 Thursday

Moon in Scorpio
Moon enters Sagittarius 10:44 pm

7 Friday

Moon in Sagittarius

8 Saturday

Moon in Sagittarius
Moon enters Capricorn 11:11 pm

9 Sunday
Moon in Capricorn

10 Monday
Moon in Capricorn
New Moon 7:03 am
Moon enters Aquarius 10:07 pm

11 Tuesday
Moon in Aquarius

12 Wednesday
Moon in Aquarius
Moon enters Pisces 9:50 pm

13 Thursday
Moon in Pisces

14 Friday
Moon in Pisces

15 Saturday
Moon in Pisces
Moon enters Aries 12:27 am

16 Sunday
Moon in Aries

17 Monday
Moon in Aries
Second Quarter 1:57 am
Moon enters Taurus 7:06 am

Birthday of Martin Luther King, Jr. (observed)

18 Tuesday
Moon in Taurus

19 Wednesday
Moon in Taurus
Moon enters Gemini 5:24 pm
Sun enters Aquarius 6:22 pm

20 Thursday
Moon in Gemini

Inauguration Day

21 Friday
Moon in Gemini

22 Saturday
Moon in Gemini
Moon enters Cancer 5:42 am

23 Sunday
Moon in Cancer

24 Monday
Moon in Cancer
Moon enters Leo 6:21 pm

25 Tuesday
Moon in Leo
Full Moon 5:32 am

26 Wednesday
Moon in Leo

27 Thursday
Moon in Leo
Moon enters Virgo 6:24 am

28 Friday
Moon in Virgo

29 Saturday
Moon in Virgo
Moon enters Libra 5:13 pm

30 Sunday
Moon in Libra

31 Monday
Moon in Libra

1 Tuesday
Moon in Libra
Moon enters Scorpio 1:51 am

2 Wednesday
Moon in Scorpio
Fourth Quarter 2:27 am

Imbolc ✦ Groundhog Day

3 Thursday
Moon in Scorpio
Moon enters Sagittarius 7:21 am

4 Friday
Moon in Sagittarius

5 Saturday
Moon in Sagittarius
Moon enters Capricorn 9:32 am

6 Sunday
Moon in Capricorn

7 Monday
Moon in Capricorn
Moon enters Aquarius 9:26 am

8 Tuesday
Moon in Aquarius
New Moon 5:28 pm

Mardi Gras

9 Wednesday
Moon in Aquarius
Moon enters Pisces 8:59 am

Ash Wednesday ◆ Chinese New Year (rooster)

10 Thursday
Moon in Pisces

Islamic New Year

11 Friday
Moon in Pisces
Moon enters Aries 10:21 am

12 Saturday
Moon in Aries

13 Sunday

Moon in Aries
Moon enters Taurus 3:18 pm

14 Monday

Moon in Taurus

Valentine's Day

15 Tuesday

Moon in Taurus
Second Quarter 7:16 pm

16 Wednesday

Moon in Taurus
Moon enters Gemini 12:18 am

17 Thursday

Moon in Gemini

18 Friday

Moon in Gemini
Sun enters Pisces 8:32 am
Moon enters Cancer 12:13 pm

19 Saturday

Moon in Cancer

20 Sunday
Moon in Cancer

21 Monday
Moon in Cancer
Moon enters Leo 12:54 am

Presidents' Day (observed)

22 Tuesday
Moon in Leo

23 Wednesday
Moon in Leo
Moon enters Virgo 12:44 pm
Full Moon 11:54 pm

24 Thursday
Moon in Virgo

25 Friday
Moon in Virgo
Moon enters Libra 10:59 pm

26 Saturday
Moon in Libra

27 Sunday
Moon in Libra

28 Monday
Moon in Libra
Moon enters Scorpio 7:21 am

1 Tuesday
Moon in Scorpio

2 Wednesday
Moon in Scorpio
Moon enters Sagittarius 1:29 pm

3 Thursday
Moon in Sagittarius
Fourth Quarter 12:36 pm

4 Friday
Moon in Sagittarius
Moon enters Capricorn 5:12 pm

5 Saturday
Moon in Capricorn

6 Sunday

Moon in Capricorn
Moon enters Aquarius 6:49 pm

7 Monday

Moon in Aquarius

8 Tuesday

Moon in Aquarius
Moon enters Pisces 7:32 pm

9 Wednesday

Moon in Pisces

10 Thursday

Moon in Pisces
New Moon 4:10 am
Moon enters Aries 9:03 pm

11 Friday

Moon in Aries

12 Saturday

Moon in Aries

13 Sunday

Moon in Aries
Moon enters Taurus 1:05 am

14 Monday

Moon in Taurus

15 Tuesday

Moon in Taurus
Moon enters Gemini 8:44 am

16 Wednesday

Moon in Gemini

17 Thursday

Moon in Gemini
Second Quarter 2:19 pm
Moon enters Cancer 7:44 pm

St. Patrick's Day

18 Friday

Moon in Cancer

19 Saturday

Moon in Cancer

20 Sunday

Moon in Cancer
Sun enters Aries 7:33 am
Moon enters Leo 8:17 am

Ostara ✦ Palm Sunday

21 Monday

Moon in Leo

22 Tuesday

Moon in Leo
Moon enters Virgo 8:10 pm

23 Wednesday

Moon in Virgo

24 Thursday

Moon in Virgo

25 Friday

Moon in Virgo
Moon enters Libra 6:00 am
Full Moon 3:58 pm

Good Friday ✦ Purim

26 Saturday

Moon in Libra

27 Sunday

Moon in Libra
Moon enters Scorpio 1:29 pm

Easter

28 Monday

Moon in Scorpio

29 Tuesday

Moon in Scorpio
Moon enters Sagittarius 6:56 pm

30 Wednesday

Moon in Sagittarius

31 Thursday

Moon in Sagittarius
Moon enters Capricorn 10:48 pm

1 Friday

Moon in Capricorn
Fourth Quarter 7:50 pm

April Fools' Day

2 Saturday

Moon in Capricorn

3 Sunday

Moon in Capricorn
Moon enters Aquarius 1:31 am

Daylight Saving Time begins at 2 am

4 Monday

Moon in Aquarius

5 Tuesday

Moon in Aquarius
Moon enters Pisces 4:45 am

6 Wednesday

Moon in Pisces

7 Thursday

Moon in Pisces
Moon enters Aries 7:28 am

8 Friday

Moon in Aries
New Moon 4:32 pm

9 Saturday

Moon in Aries
Moon enters Taurus 11:50 am

10 Sunday

Moon in Taurus

11 Monday

Moon in Taurus
Moon enters Gemini 6:55 pm

12 Tuesday

Moon in Gemini

13 Wednesday

Moon in Gemini

14 Thursday

Moon in Gemini
Moon enters Cancer 5:03 am

15 Friday

Moon in Cancer

16 Saturday

Moon in Cancer
Second Quarter 10:37 am
Moon enters Leo 5:17 pm

17 Sunday
Moon in Leo

18 Monday
Moon in Leo

19 Tuesday
Moon in Leo
Moon enters Virgo 5:27 am
Sun enters Taurus 7:37 pm

20 Wednesday
Moon in Virgo

21 Thursday
Moon in Virgo
Moon enters Libra 3:27 pm

22 Friday
Moon in Libra

Earth Day
23 Saturday
Moon in Libra
Moon enters Scorpio 10:25 pm

24 Sunday
Moon in Scorpio
Full Moon 6:06 am

Passover begins

25 Monday
Moon in Scorpio

26 Tuesday
Moon in Scorpio
Moon enters Sagittarius 2:46 am

27 Wednesday
Moon in Sagittarius

28 Thursday
Moon in Sagittarius
Moon enters Capricorn 5:33 am

29 Friday
Moon in Capricorn

Orthodox Good Friday

30 Saturday
Moon in Capricorn
Moon enters Aquarius 7:54 am

Passover ends

1 Sunday

Moon in Aquarius
Fourth Quarter 2:24 am

Beltane ✦ Orthodox Easter

2 Monday

Moon in Aquarius
Moon enters Pisces 10:43 am

3 Tuesday

Moon in Pisces

4 Wednesday

Moon in Pisces
Moon enters Aries 2:36 pm

5 Thursday

Moon in Aries

Cinco de Mayo

6 Friday

Moon in Aries
Moon enters Taurus 8:01 pm

7 Saturday

Moon in Taurus

8 Sunday
Moon in Taurus
New Moon 4:45 am

Mother's Day

9 Monday
Moon in Taurus
Moon enters Gemini 3:29 am

10 Tuesday
Moon in Gemini

11 Wednesday
Moon in Gemini
Moon enters Cancer 1:20 pm

12 Thursday
Moon in Cancer

13 Friday
Moon in Cancer

14 Saturday
Moon in Cancer
Moon enters Leo 1:17 am

15 Sunday
Moon in Leo

16 Monday
Moon in Leo
Second Quarter 4:57 am
Moon enters Virgo 1:46 pm

17 Tuesday
Moon in Virgo

18 Wednesday
Moon in Virgo

19 Thursday
Moon in Virgo
Moon enters Libra 12:30 am

20 Friday
Moon in Libra
Sun enters Gemini 6:47 pm

21 Saturday
Moon in Libra
Moon enters Scorpio 7:49 am

22 Sunday
Moon in Scorpio

23 Monday
Moon in Scorpio
Moon enters Sagittarius 11:38 am
Full Moon 4:18 pm

24 Tuesday
Moon in Sagittarius

25 Wednesday
Moon in Sagittarius
Moon enters Capricorn 1:11 pm

26 Thursday
Moon in Capricorn

27 Friday
Moon in Capricorn
Moon enters Aquarius 2:10 pm

28 Saturday
Moon in Aquarius

29 Sunday
Moon in Aquarius
Moon enters Pisces 4:09 pm

30 Monday
Moon in Pisces
Fourth Quarter 7:47 am

Memorial Day (observed)

31 Tuesday
Moon in Pisces
Moon enters Aries 8:07 pm

1 Wednesday
Moon in Aries

2 Thursday
Moon in Aries

3 Friday
Moon in Aries
Moon enters Taurus 2:20 am

4 Saturday
Moon in Taurus

5 Sunday

Moon in Taurus
Moon enters Gemini 10:36 am

6 Monday

Moon in Gemini
New Moon 5:55 pm

7 Tuesday

Moon in Gemini
Moon enters Cancer 8:46 pm

8 Wednesday

Moon in Cancer

9 Thursday

Moon in Cancer

10 Friday

Moon in Cancer
Moon enters Leo 8:39 am

11 Saturday

Moon in Leo

---

12 Sunday

Moon in Leo
Moon enters Virgo 9:22 pm

---

13 Monday

Moon in Virgo

Shavuot

14 Tuesday

Moon in Virgo
Second Quarter 9:22 pm

Flag Day

15 Wednesday

Moon in Virgo
Moon enters Libra 8:59 am

---

16 Thursday

Moon in Libra

---

17 Friday

Moon in Libra
Moon enters Scorpio 5:23 pm

---

18 Saturday

Moon in Scorpio

---

19 Sunday

Moon in Scorpio
Moon enters Sagittarius 9:45 pm

Pentecost ♦ Father's Day

20 Monday

Moon in Sagittarius

21 Tuesday

Moon in Sagittarius
Sun enters Cancer 2:46 am
Moon enters Capricorn 10:52 pm

Litha

22 Wednesday

Moon in Capricorn
Full Moon 12:14 am

23 Thursday

Moon in Capricorn
Moon enters Aquarius 10:36 pm

24 Friday

Moon in Aquarius

25 Saturday

Moon in Aquarius
Moon enters Pisces 11:03 pm

26 Sunday
Moon in Pisces

27 Monday
Moon in Pisces

28 Tuesday
Moon in Pisces
Moon enters Aries 1:51 am
Fourth Quarter 2:23 pm

29 Wednesday
Moon in Aries

30 Thursday
Moon in Aries
Moon enters Taurus 7:45 am

1 Friday
Moon in Taurus

2 Saturday
Moon in Taurus
Moon enters Gemini 4:26 pm

3 Sunday
Moon in Gemini

4 Monday
Moon in Gemini

Independence Day

5 Tuesday
Moon in Gemini
Moon enters Cancer 3:07 am

6 Wednesday
Moon in Cancer
New Moon 8:02 am

7 Thursday
Moon in Cancer
Moon enters Leo 3:11 pm

8 Friday
Moon in Leo

9 Saturday
Moon in Leo

10 Sunday

Moon in Leo
Moon enters Virgo 3:57 am

11 Monday

Moon in Virgo

12 Tuesday

Moon in Virgo
Moon enters Libra 4:09 pm

13 Wednesday

Moon in Libra

14 Thursday

Moon in Libra
Second Quarter 11:20 am

15 Friday

Moon in Libra
Moon enters Scorpio 1:51 am

16 Saturday

Moon in Scorpio

17 Sunday

Moon in Scorpio
Moon enters Sagittarius 7:35 am

18 Monday

Moon in Sagittarius

19 Tuesday

Moon in Sagittarius
Moon enters Capricorn 9:26 am

20 Wednesday

Moon in Capricorn

21 Thursday

Moon in Capricorn
Full Moon 7:00 am
Moon enters Aquarius 8:55 am

22 Friday

Moon in Aquarius
Sun enters Leo 1:41 pm

23 Saturday

Moon in Aquarius
Moon enters Pisces 8:12 am

24 Sunday
Moon in Pisces

25 Monday
Moon in Pisces
Moon enters Aries 9:23 am

26 Tuesday
Moon in Aries

27 Wednesday
Moon in Aries
Moon enters Taurus 1:54 pm
Fourth Quarter 11:19 pm

28 Thursday
Moon in Taurus

29 Friday
Moon in Taurus
Moon enters Gemini 10:02 pm

30 Saturday
Moon in Gemini

31 Sunday
Moon in Gemini

1 Monday
Moon in Gemini
Moon enters Cancer 8:52 am

Lammas

2 Tuesday
Moon in Cancer

3 Wednesday
Moon in Cancer
Moon enters Leo 9:10 pm

4 Thursday
Moon in Leo
New Moon 11:05 pm

5 Friday
Moon in Leo

6 Saturday
Moon in Leo
Moon enters Virgo 9:54 am

7 Sunday
Moon in Virgo

8 Monday
Moon in Virgo
Moon enters Libra 10:08 pm

9 Tuesday
Moon in Libra

10 Wednesday
Moon in Libra

11 Thursday
Moon in Libra
Moon enters Scorpio 8:35 am

12 Friday
Moon in Scorpio
Second Quarter 10:38 pm

13 Saturday
Moon in Scorpio
Moon enters Sagittarius 3:47 pm

14 Sunday
Moon in Sagittarius

15 Monday
Moon in Sagittarius
Moon enters Capricorn 7:13 pm

16 Tuesday
Moon in Capricorn

17 Wednesday
Moon in Capricorn
Moon enters Aquarius 7:39 pm

18 Thursday
Moon in Aquarius

19 Friday
Moon in Aquarius
Full Moon 1:53 pm
Moon enters Pisces 6:52 pm

20 Saturday
Moon in Pisces

21 Sunday
Moon in Pisces
Moon enters Aries 7:01 pm

22 Monday
Moon in Aries
Sun enters Virgo 8:45 pm

23 Tuesday
Moon in Aries
Moon enters Taurus 9:58 pm

24 Wednesday
Moon in Taurus

25 Thursday
Moon in Taurus

26 Friday
Moon in Taurus
Moon enters Gemini 4:43 am
Fourth Quarter 11:18 am

27 Saturday
Moon in Gemini

28 Sunday
Moon in Gemini
Moon enters Cancer 2:57 pm

29 Monday
Moon in Cancer

30 Tuesday
Moon in Cancer

31 Wednesday
Moon in Cancer
Moon enters Leo 3:14 am

1 Thursday
Moon in Leo

2 Friday
Moon in Leo
Moon enters Virgo 3:56 pm

3 Saturday
Moon in Virgo
New Moon 2:45 pm

4 Sunday
Moon in Virgo

5 Monday
Moon in Virgo
Moon enters Libra 3:52 am

Labor Day

6 Tuesday
Moon in Libra

7 Wednesday
Moon in Libra
Moon enters Scorpio 2:10 pm

8 Thursday
Moon in Scorpio

9 Friday
Moon in Scorpio
Moon enters Sagittarius 10:03 pm

10 Saturday
Moon in Sagittarius

11 Sunday

Moon in Sagittarius
Second Quarter 7:37 am

12 Monday

Moon in Sagittarius
Moon enters Capricorn 2:56 am

13 Tuesday

Moon in Capricorn

14 Wednesday

Moon in Capricorn
Moon enters Aquarius 5:02 am

15 Thursday

Moon in Aquarius

16 Friday

Moon in Aquarius
Moon enters Pisces 5:24 am

17 Saturday

Moon in Pisces
Full Moon 10:01 pm

18 Sunday
Moon in Pisces
Moon enters Aries 5:43 am

19 Monday
Moon in Aries

20 Tuesday
Moon in Aries
Moon enters Taurus 7:47 am

21 Wednesday
Moon in Taurus

22 Thursday
Moon in Taurus
Moon enters Gemini 1:07 pm
Sun enters Libra 6:23 pm

Mabon

23 Friday
Moon in Gemini

24 Saturday
Moon in Gemini
Moon enters Cancer 10:10 pm

25 Sunday
Moon in Cancer
Fourth Quarter 2:41 am

26 Monday
Moon in Cancer

27 Tuesday
Moon in Cancer
Moon enters Leo 10:03 am

28 Wednesday
Moon in Leo

29 Thursday
Moon in Leo
Moon enters Virgo 10:44 pm

30 Friday
Moon in Virgo

1 Saturday
Moon in Virgo

2 Sunday

Moon in Virgo
Moon enters Libra 10:24 am

3 Monday

Moon in Libra
New Moon 6:28 am

4 Tuesday

Moon in Libra
Moon enters Scorpio 8:03 pm

Ramadan begins ◆ Rosh Hashanah

5 Wednesday

Moon in Scorpio

6 Thursday

Moon in Scorpio

7 Friday

Moon in Scorpio
Moon enters Sagittarius 3:28 am

8 Saturday

Moon in Sagittarius

9 Sunday

Moon in Sagittarius
Moon enters Capricorn 8:43 am

10 Monday

Moon in Capricorn
Second Quarter 3:01 pm

Columbus Day (observed)

11 Tuesday

Moon in Capricorn
Moon enters Aquarius 12:05 pm

12 Wednesday

Moon in Aquarius

13 Thursday

Moon in Aquarius
Moon enters Pisces 2:05 pm

Yom Kippur

14 Friday

Moon in Pisces

15 Saturday

Moon in Pisces
Moon enters Aries 3:39 pm

16 Sunday
Moon in Aries

17 Monday
Moon in Aries
Full Moon 8:14 am
Moon enters Taurus 6:04 pm

18 Tuesday
Moon in Taurus

Sukkot begins

19 Wednesday
Moon in Taurus
Moon enters Gemini 10:44 pm

20 Thursday
Moon in Gemini

21 Friday
Moon in Gemini

22 Saturday
Moon in Gemini
Moon enters Cancer 6:41 am

23 Sunday

Moon in Cancer
Sun enters Scorpio 3:42 am

24 Monday

Moon in Cancer
Moon enters Leo 5:48 pm
Fourth Quarter 9:17 pm

Sukkot ends

25 Tuesday

Moon in Leo

26 Wednesday

Moon in Leo

27 Thursday

Moon in Leo
Moon enters Virgo 6:28 am

28 Friday

Moon in Virgo

29 Saturday

Moon in Virgo
Moon enters Libra 6:15 pm

30 Sunday
Moon in Libra

Daylight Saving Time ends at 2 am

31 Monday
Moon in Libra

Halloween/Samhain

1 Tuesday
Moon in Libra
Moon enters Scorpio 2:29 am
New Moon 8:25 pm

All Saints' Day

2 Wednesday
Moon in Scorpio

3 Thursday
Moon in Scorpio
Moon enters Sagittarius 8:55 am

Ramadan ends

4 Friday
Moon in Sagittarius

5 Saturday
Moon in Sagittarius
Moon enters Capricorn 1:17 pm

6 Sunday

Moon in Capricorn

7 Monday

Moon in Capricorn
Moon enters Aquarius 4:31 pm

8 Tuesday

Moon in Aquarius
Second Quarter 8:57 pm

Election Day

9 Wednesday

Moon in Aquarius
Moon enters Pisces 7:22 pm

10 Thursday

Moon in Pisces

11 Friday

Moon in Pisces
Moon enters Aries 10:22 pm

Veterans Day

12 Saturday

Moon in Aries

13 Sunday
Moon in Aries

14 Monday
Moon in Aries
Moon enters Taurus 2:02 am

15 Tuesday
Moon in Taurus
Full Moon 7:58 pm

16 Wednesday
Moon in Taurus
Moon enters Gemini 7:10 am

17 Thursday
Moon in Gemini

18 Friday
Moon in Gemini
Moon enters Cancer 2:42 pm

19 Saturday
Moon in Cancer

20 Sunday
Moon in Cancer

21 Monday
Moon in Cancer
Moon enters Leo 1:10 am

22 Tuesday
Moon in Leo
Sun enters Sagittarius 12:15 am

23 Wednesday
Moon in Leo
Moon enters Virgo 1:41 pm
Fourth Quarter 5:11 pm

24 Thursday
Moon in Virgo

Thanksgiving Day

25 Friday
Moon in Virgo

26 Saturday
Moon in Virgo
Moon enters Libra 1:58 am

27 Sunday
Moon in Libra

28 Monday
Moon in Libra
Moon enters Scorpio 11:33 am

29 Tuesday
Moon in Scorpio

30 Wednesday
Moon in Scorpio
Moon enters Sagittarius 5:32 pm

1 Thursday
Moon in Sagittarius
New Moon 10:01 am

2 Friday
Moon in Sagittarius
Moon enters Capricorn 8:42 pm

3 Saturday
Moon in Capricorn

---

4 Sunday
Moon in Capricorn
Moon enters Aquarius 10:36 pm

---

5 Monday
Moon in Aquarius

---

6 Tuesday
Moon in Aquarius

---

7 Wednesday
Moon in Aquarius
Moon enters Pisces 12:44 am

---

8 Thursday
Moon in Pisces
Second Quarter 4:36 am

---

9 Friday
Moon in Pisces
Moon enters Aries 4:02 am

---

10 Saturday
Moon in Aries

---

11 Sunday

Moon in Aries
Moon enters Taurus 8:46 am

12 Monday

Moon in Taurus

13 Tuesday

Moon in Taurus
Moon enters Gemini 2:59 pm

14 Wednesday

Moon in Gemini

15 Thursday

Moon in Gemini
Full Moon 11:16 am
Moon enters Cancer 11:01 pm

16 Friday

Moon in Cancer

17 Saturday

Moon in Cancer

18 Sunday

Moon in Cancer
Moon enters Leo 9:18 am

19 Monday

Moon in Leo

20 Tuesday

Moon in Leo
Moon enters Virgo 9:39 pm

21 Wednesday

Moon in Virgo
Sun enters Capricorn 1:35 pm

Yule

22 Thursday

Moon in Virgo

23 Friday

Moon in Virgo
Moon enters Libra 10:26 am
Fourth Quarter 2:36 pm

24 Saturday

Moon in Libra

Christmas Eve

25 Sunday

Moon in Libra
Moon enters Scorpio 9:04 pm

Christmas Day

26 Monday

Moon in Scorpio

Hanukkah begins ✦ Kwanzaa begins

27 Tuesday

Moon in Scorpio

28 Wednesday

Moon in Scorpio
Moon enters Sagittarius 3:43 am

29 Thursday

Moon in Sagittarius

30 Friday

Moon in Sagittarius
Moon enters Capricorn 6:35 am
New Moon 10:12 pm

31 Saturday

Moon in Capricorn

New Year's Eve

1 Sunday

Moon in Capricorn
Moon enters Aquarius 7:14 am

New Year's Day ♦ Kwanzaa ends

2 Monday

Moon in Aquarius

Hanukkah ends

3 Tuesday

Moon in Aquarius
Moon enters Pisces 7:43 am

4 Wednesday

Moon in Pisces

5 Thursday

Moon in Pisces
Moon enters Aries 9:44 am

6 Friday

Moon in Aries
Second Quarter 1:56 pm

7 Saturday

Moon in Aries
Moon enters Taurus 2:09 pm

The Year 2006

January

S	M	T	W	T	F	S
1	2	3	4	5	6	7
8	9	10	11	12	13	14
15	16	17	18	19	20	21
22	23	24	25	26	27	28
29	30	31				

February

S	M	T	W	T	F	S
			1	2	3	4
5	6	7	8	9	10	11
12	13	14	15	16	17	18
19	20	21	22	23	24	25
26	27	28				

March

S	M	T	W	T	F	S
			1	2	3	4
5	6	7	8	9	10	11
12	13	14	15	16	17	18
19	20	21	22	23	24	25
26	27	28	29	30	31	

April

S	M	T	W	T	F	S
						1
2	3	4	5	6	7	8
9	10	11	12	13	14	15
16	17	18	19	20	21	22
23	24	25	26	27	28	29
30						

May

S	M	T	W	T	F	S
	1	2	3	4	5	6
7	8	9	10	11	12	13
14	15	16	17	18	19	20
21	22	23	24	25	26	27
28	29	30	31			

June

S	M	T	W	T	F	S
				1	2	3
4	5	6	7	8	9	10
11	12	13	14	15	16	17
18	19	20	21	22	23	24
25	26	27	28	29	30	

July

S	M	T	W	T	F	S
						1
2	3	4	5	6	7	8
9	10	11	12	13	14	15
16	17	18	19	20	21	22
23	24	25	26	27	28	29
30	31					

August

S	M	T	W	T	F	S
		1	2	3	4	5
6	7	8	9	10	11	12
13	14	15	16	17	18	19
20	21	22	23	24	25	26
27	28	29	30	31		

September

S	M	T	W	T	F	S
					1	2
3	4	5	6	7	8	9
10	11	12	13	14	15	16
17	18	19	20	21	22	23
24	25	26	27	28	29	30

October

S	M	T	W	T	F	S
1	2	3	4	5	6	7
8	9	10	11	12	13	14
15	16	17	18	19	20	21
22	23	24	25	26	27	28
29	30	31				

November

S	M	T	W	T	F	S
			1	2	3	4
5	6	7	8	9	10	11
12	13	14	15	16	17	18
19	20	21	22	23	24	25
26	27	28	29	30		

December

S	M	T	W	T	F	S
					1	2
3	4	5	6	7	8	9
10	11	12	13	14	15	16
17	18	19	20	21	22	23
24	25	26	27	28	29	30
31						

The Hermit

For Further Study

L'EREMITA
L'ERMITE
IX
THE HERMIT
EL ERMITAÑO

DER EREMIT
DE KLUIZENAAR

Tarot and Dreams

by Diane Wilkes

Tarot and dream explication have a lot in common. The pictures on tarot cards and the images you see in your dreams offer visual metaphors that echo, illustrate, and weave together the strands of your subconscious. Both dreams and the tarot also provide information that allow you to explore and illuminate various aspects of your life on many levels.

Life As a Dream

Buddhism teaches that all life is dreams, so, by viewing life as a living dream, you can use some of the methods described in this article to explore daily incidents that strongly affect you. Perceiving all experiences as dreams helps you to avoid attaching yourself overmuch to outcome. If you do these tarot exercises for both your waking and sleeping dreams, your ability to approach both with serenity will improve. Petty personal annoyances will be shown as the temporal ephemera they are, allowing you to prioritize and focus on what really matters to you.

Finding and Creating Dreamwork Resources

Because dreams are so image oriented, it's important that you choose at least one tarot deck that appeals to you both aestheti-

cally and symbolically. If your present deck doesn't, there are hundreds of others from which to choose. You may have one deck for dreams dealing with spiritual issues and another for health concerns. Examining and ingesting various artists' vision of a particular archetype can only enrich your understanding of it.

There are numerous dream dictionaries which offer you interpretations of the various symbols that appear in your dreams. My favorite is Betty Bethards' *The Dream Book: Symbols for Self Understanding*, which not only contains a spiritually oriented dictionary but also has some excellent suggestions on how to interpret and work with your dreams. However, creating your own symbolic dictionary adds vitality and relevance to your dreamwork and supersedes any other interpretational source. Bethards may suggest apples are a "healthful influence," but if you once got drunk on Boone's Farm Apple Wine and retched for three hours, your subconscious likely perceives apples quite differently.

Programming Your Dream

There are many ways to combine tarot with dreamwork (or dreamplay). An easy one is to program your dreams with a particular tarot card that has the qualities you seek to explore in your nocturnal reveries. Select a card that reflects what you wish to dream about by going through your deck and finding an image that speaks to that topic in some way. If, for example, you want to dream about a potential lover, you could choose the Lovers card or a court card that has the qualities you seek in a partner. Meditate on the card before you go to sleep and say aloud what you wish to dream about, incorporating your thoughts about the card into your statement as a way of priming your subconscious. Place the card under your pillow and go to sleep with it as the last image in your psyche. You may wish to do this for several nights, perhaps "charging" a series of dreams to more fully explore all the elements of your question.

If you want to examine your career goals, you might choose a card that depicts the kind of work you're considering. Be creative here. While there may not be a card that identically illustrates your question, you can use the elemental correspondences to create a close-enough fit. For instance, the Three and the Eight of Pentacles both show different aspects of work, and they can be used if nothing else seems appropriate. Which do you see as the master craftsperson, and which the apprentice? Choose the card that fits your needs.

If you're considering taking a part-time job as a bartender, the Seven of Cups might aid you in making a decision. Or perhaps you'd like some help in detaching from the mental stresses of your job: the Queen of Swords can probably offer some pointed suggestions. While I offer some specific possibilities, trust your perception of your particular deck's imagery. What resonates with your psyche is most important when it comes to dreamwork and the tarot.

Recording Your Dream

The most important first step is writing down and dating your dream upon awakening. Once you establish that step as a regular morning practice, it is no more overwhelming than brushing your teeth. You can always return to the dream later, but if you don't write it down as soon as you get up you are likely to omit and/or forget something important when you try to recall it later in the day. The first thing I do each morning is go to my computer and type up my dream from the night before. You might prefer recording your dreams in a journal that you keep by your bed—or even use a tape recorder, speaking your dream into it as soon as you awaken. Make sure you date your dream so that you have a record to note patterns and precognitive messages.

Four Levels of Interpretation

I find it helpful to use the four suits/elements of the tarot as a grid for just some of the ways in which we can gain understanding into ourselves using dreams (and the tarot):

Wands/Fire—Looking at a reading or a dream for its spiritual message, or as a way to understand what truly "fires" your soul.

Cups/Water—Looking at a reading or a dream for its emotional content so that you can explore your feelings. Often we have conflicting sentiments, or our feelings and beliefs conflict with one another. Dreams and tarot spreads have a way of addressing these discordances.

Swords/Air—Looking at a reading or a dream for its intellectual or analytical properties in order to determine how it reflects your thoughts and beliefs on an issue. Determining personal and collective references also comes under the aegis of Swords/Air.

Pentacles/Earth—Looking at a reading or a dream for its divinatory, magical, or predictive messages. Assuming you make no behavioral changes, is the dream/spread offering you a physical depiction of the future? Change and free will are always available to you, but we can uncover unknown or hidden facts in the now and get a literal glimpse of what is to be via dreams and card readings.

Interpreting the Dream

Interpretation is a word often used in terms of both dreams and tarot, but don't let that word limit you. Often, there is no one "correct" interpretation, but a range of insights that you can glean from a dream and/or a tarot reading. Words like "illumination," "exploration," and "explication" are all valid concepts that allow you to seek multiple revelations.

Gail Fairfield offers a simple and effective way of using the tarot to interpret a dream in her classic work, *Everyday Tarot: A Choice Centered Book*. She recommends that you break down and number your dream into simple sentences, such as in the following example:

1. I walk in the door and a monster awaits.
2. He is huge and wears a Superman uniform that is too tight for his oversized green body.
3. He screams, "I have been waiting for you to bring the Kryptonite for days!"

You then randomly select a card for each numbered portion of your dream and use it to bring insight into its meaning for you. Let's say you pulled the Two of Pentacles for the first sentence. We'll look at it from the four-element perspective mentioned above. On a Wands/Fire level, you could feel like you are on spiritual overload, possibly from discovering a new path or a recent initiation ("I walk in the door"). From a Cups/Water perspective, you could feel overwhelmed by your "monstrous" schedule, a schedule you can't seem to balance. Using the airy Swords approach, you might think you are cruising for a challenging, intellectual bruising. On the Pentacles/Earth level, you could perceive a new responsibility is going to be more daunting than you initially believed.

Of course, you don't have to approach each card from every

level. Gleaning a single insight from each card is often enough to provide a great deal of guidance.

An In-Depth Process

You can combine tarot with your dreamwork as simply or with as much complexity as you'd like. Here's a rather lengthy psychological process that will help you deeply explore the significance of your dreams:

1. Date and record your dream, using as much detail as you can remember.

2. Make three lists:
   a) the people appearing in your dream (including yourself),
   b) the items that appeared in your dream (a house, a car, a bed, etc.), and
   c) the actions/occurrences (going to the park, flying, etc.), which can be found by listing the verbs.

3. Separate your deck into two sections:
   a) court cards, and
   b) the Major and Minor Arcana.

4. Pull a card from the court card section of the deck for each of the people who appeared in your dream; pull a card from the remainder of the deck for each item in the other two lists. Any Major Arcana cards drawn indicate that the item or action is emphasized and requires special attention. The card's archetypal meaning will suggest the theme and nature of your dream.

5. Write up what you think each card means in relation to the components of your dream.

6. Go through the deck with conscious intent (that is, by looking faceup at the pictures on the cards) and find the card that expresses the feelings you had as you awoke from the dream, or that you have now regarding the dream. Record this card and a brief explanation of what it means to you in this context.

7. Go through the deck with conscious intent and select the card that most defines what you think the dream means. Record this card and a brief explanation of what it means to you in this context.

8. Go through the deck with conscious intent and select the card that suggests an action you might take to "make your dream come true" (if desired) or to ameliorate any negative behaviors you feel the dream indicates. Record this card, as well as the necessary action and when you plan to do this action.

9. Return all the cards to the deck, shuffle, and choose one card. This card indicates the secret, unexplained part of the dream. If the card is one that has already been a part of this process, it indicates that, while you have a very good handle on your dream, this particular card has a special meaning and, perhaps, has suggestions, interpretations, and solutions to offer you. You may wish to meditate on the card or carry it with you for the day in order to enrich your understanding.

The suggestions above form an ideal scenario that assumes you have plenty of time to work with your dream. But the process does not have to be quite so time-consuming. Even a simple one-card pull to understand your dream as a whole will often give you sufficient direction, which you can expand upon at a later date, if you so choose.

Dreaming Tarot Spreads

Years ago I actually dreamed a tarot spread. I was reacting badly to someone I had considered a friend who was spending the night at my home. I dreamt that I did a reading about her that clarified my discomfort with her. When I awakened, I wrote down the spread as I remembered it, and have since found it helpful to use whenever I'm feeling conflicting emotions about someone.

You don't have to specifically dream about a spread in order to use it as the basis of a layout, though. If the dream is similar to a story, you can break the dream into parts. Using the three-sentence sample dream I used earlier to illustrate Fairfield's method, I have turned each image into a question to create the following spread:

Card One: What is the door (block/barrier)?
Card Two: What do I fear is behind the door? (the monster)
Card Three: How does it overwhelm me? (the monster's size)
Card Four: What constricts me? (the fit of the monster's attire)
Card Five: What would allow me to grow? (the color green)
Card Six: What unpaid debt do I owe? (the overdue Kryptonite)

I should mention that, while I made up this dream off the top of my head to illustrate a specific method, the spread I created turned out to be quite relevant for me personally. The implicit, greater teaching of this story is that our subconscious is a rich resource for exploring what we can't or don't always access in other ways.

Dreams and tarot can be used as tools that bridge the subconscious and the conscious, and, like the Hermit's lantern, shed illumination so that we can walk a path of enlightened awareness.

A Closer Look At:

Waking the Wild Spirit Tarot

Created and illustrated by Poppy Palin

- 78 full-color cards and a 312-page illustrated book

- Cards are 4⅝ x 3¼, with nonreversible backs and illustrated pips

- Nontraditional correspondences create an entirely new set of archetypes to help you explore the tarot

- Vibrant artwork is based on traditional Pagan imagery, storybook characters, and mythic archetypes

- Illustrated book explains each card through a first-person story narrated by the card's character

Comparative Tarot

by Bonnie Cehovet

The tarot is a wonderful tool, rich in archetypal content and visual symbolism. It helps us to bring life into focus—giving breadth and depth to our visions, clarity to our goals, and purpose to our actions. Working with the soul of tarot brings us closer to becoming whole, to living from the core of our being.

The tarot has many layers; as we access each layer, we become more and more aware of who we are, of what lessons we are here to learn, and how they tie into our purpose for this lifetime. The wisdom contained within the tarot can be accessed in many ways: some of the more traditional methods are the use of tarot spreads, meditation, the creation of mandalas, journaling, and the creation of ritual. What each of these methods has in common is the use of the tarot cards as a visual focus.

The visual focus of the cards will change from deck to deck, since each deck carries its own theme and reflects its own highly individualized concept of the qualities inherent in each card. One way to access the depth of wisdom that is tarot is to make the conscious choice to work with decks that have disparate themes and symbology, that bring out the wisdom of the cards in very different ways.

Done indiscriminately, this approach can lead to chaos: too many concepts, too many ideas, too many paths to follow. However, there is a disciplined approach to using multiple decks for study: it is termed comparative tarot. Here the reader is, in a very literal manner, comparing diverse tarot decks card for card.

What do we gain from the comparative tarot approach?

- A greater understanding and appreciation of the intent of the artist for each deck
- An appreciation for the uses of astrological, numerological, and alchemical symbols
- An appreciation for the use of color and different media in the creation of the cards
- A greater understanding of and appreciation for the imagery in each of the cards
- A greater understanding of and appreciation for where the symbols and imagery of the tarot come from
- A greater understanding of how the archetypal imagery of the tarot and our myths and legends reflect each other

What a marvelous way to gently wander into that "aha!" experience that takes our understanding of tarot to a whole new level!

The Comparative Method

So—exactly what is comparative tarot and how do we work with it? First we place the cards from one deck out for study, whether in the form of a tarot spread or by using one or more cards for meditation, journaling, mandala work, or ceremony creation. The cards are read and impressions noted using whichever method appeals to the reader (written journaling, electronic journaling, taping, or some other method). Then a second, comparative deck is chosen. The same cards that were drawn from the primary deck are drawn from the comparative deck, and the cards are placed side by side for comparison and study.

In order to use the comparative tarot approach to best advantage, the reader should have a primary deck to work with. He or she should have a fairly in-depth understanding of the theme, the creator's intent, and the symbolism contained within that deck. When choosing a deck for the comparative reading, the reader should take into account the nature of the primary deck being used, the nature of the reading, and the reader's impetus for using the comparative tarot method.

The nature of the deck being used. In order to make the best use of this system, the deck chosen for the comparative reading should be different in some manner from the primary deck. If the primary deck is heavy on esoteric symbolism, a good choice for a comparative deck might be one that leans more towards the use of visual graphics. A good example here might be the *Universal Tarot* (Maxwell Miller) as a primary deck and the *Morgan Greer* (Bill Greer) as a comparative deck.

The nature of the reading. If the reading is of a highly spiritual nature, then decks that are essentially "fun" would not add any depth of understanding. However, a comparative deck that also carries the theme of spirituality would be of great assistance. For example, if the reading is of a spiritual nature, and the primary deck used was the *Osho Zen Tarot* (Ma Padma Deva, Osho Zen International), then a good comparative deck might be the *Shapeshifter Tarot* (D. J. Conway and Sirona Knight, illustrated by Lisa Hunt).

The reader's impetus for using the comparative tarot method. The impetus for doing a comparative reading may be simply to clarify, or add depth to, a reading. In this case, choosing a comparative deck that follows a different theme will work well. If the impetus for the use of the comparative method is to gain wisdom about a specific tarot card, then the theme of the card may be less important than the visual appeal of the card. In this case, I would take several decks out, drawing the card in question from each of them. Placing them all side by side, I would choose one or more cards for comparison and begin my study.

If the impetus for the use of the comparative method is to gain a better understanding of a specific deck, then I would use as a primary deck one that I was well versed in—whether the theme was the same or not.

Once the primary cards are laid out, the comparative deck chosen, and the comparative cards laid out, the fun begins! This is the procedure that I follow for doing a deck comparison. The procedure that each individual reader uses will be determined by what works for him or her.

- Overall impression of the layout
- Overall comparison of the themes
- Overall comparison of colors and medium
- Comparison of the use of symbolism between the decks

Comparative Tarot: An Example

The following is an example of how the comparative tarot method can be implemented:

Primary deck

Tarot of the Saints (Robert M. Place)

Comparative deck

Victoria Regina Tarot (Sarah Ovenall, Georg Patterson)

Question

How will the seeker's life change after his anticipated relocation to another state?

Spread

Three card, linear spread, placed from left to right.

Position definitions:

1. Where the seeker is at the present time
2. What the relocation will bring to the seeker

The Six of Wands from the *Tarot of the Saints*

SIX OF STAFFS

The Six of Wands from *The Victoria Regina Tarot*

Six ∘ Wands

FIVE OF COINS

The Five of Coins from the Tarot of the Saints

Five ∘ Coins

The Five of Coins from The Victoria Regina Tarot

3. How the Seeker can best integrate the energies of the relocation into his life

Cards drawn:

1. Six of Staffs (Wands) / Six of Wands
2. Five of Coins (Pentacles) / Five of Coins (Pentacles)
3. St. John—Knight of Cups / Prince (Knight) of Cups

Overall impression of the layout

The *Tarot of the Saints* carries the theme of the wisdom of the saints. The cards are done in a gentle, uncluttered manner that lend themselves to introspection and meditation. There is a sense of seriousness here, a sense of "this is what you will be experiencing, and this is how to handle it." There is a feeling here of moving from a place of being in control to a place of loneliness and despair—a place where there is little control. But in the end the seeker transcends his difficulties by listening to his subconscious, or inner self.

The *Victoria Regina Tarot* carries within it the theme of the Victorian era in an amazing collage format. Where the *Tarot of the Saints* is very "otherworldly," the *Victoria Regina Tarot* portrays the feel of the Victorian era—the down-to-earth nature of things, the history of that time period, and the way the archetypes representing human kind are played out. There is less of a sense of being "out of control," and more of a sense of responsibility for others. The "resolution" here seems much more mundane, much more easily attainable.

Overall comparison of the themes

The *Tarot of the Saints* is very much a meditative deck. The manner in which I would personally work with this deck would be on an internal level. The wisdom gained would be an understanding of myself gained through introspection.

The *Victoria Regina Tarot* retains a stronger connection to the physical plane. There is just enough fantasy in the collage work to open the mind to the world of spirit, while leaving one with the understanding that the work that needs to be done is on the physical plane.

Overall comparison of colors and medium

The *Tarot of the Saints* is done in a very stark manner: clean lines, little background, no frills. The colors are clear, but they do not overtake the graphics. They are used for symbolism more than anything else.

ST. JOHN ▪ KNIGHT OF CUPS

The Knight of Cups from the Tarot of the Saints

Prince ∘ Cups

The Prince of Cups from The Victoria Regina Tarot

The *Victoria Regina Tarot* is a black-and-white collage deck. A great deal of work has gone into bringing the right amount of whimsy into the cards, along with an extremely accurate presentation of the people and times of Queen Victoria's reign.

Comparison of the use of symbolism between the decks

The *Tarot of the Saints* is a very literal deck. The symbols are traditional and are connected with each of the saints portrayed. I found the "small" scenes on the pips—the scenes placed under the elemental symbols for the card—quite interesting.

The *Victoria Regina Tarot* uses symbolism of a more mundane nature—but it is certainly as effective as that of the *Tarot of the Saints*. In the Five of Coins, we see in the background several clocks, all showing different times. The immediate thought here is: "Where is time taking the seeker? What will happen if he pays attention to the time?"

Reading

Tarot of the Saints: The seeker is currently in a place of acceptance. He is, or feels that he is, in accordance with his environment. He has a full understanding of that which surrounds him, and feels in control. The relocation will take him out of alignment with himself—it will bring him great loneliness and a loss of his sense of self. The seeker can best align himself with his new environment by taking the time to look within, to listen to internal messages.

Victoria Regina Tarot: In this deck I get more of a sense of "victory"—that the seeker is in accord with his environment because of his own action; he is being acknowledged for work well done. This gives a more fleeting sense to the issue of control in the environment. There is also more of a feeling here that the loneliness is not self-imposed—that the seeker is feeling abandoned and in need of both emotional and "real time" support. As far as integrating the energies of the relocation into his life, the indication in this deck comes more in the form of a warning—to pay attention to what is real, to not allow fantasy to take over.

There is a very real difference between these two decks—between their themes and between the manner in which the energies of the cards are presented. Together, they blend the wisdom of the spiritual realm with the wisdom of the physical realm. This is the heart of comparative tarot—to take differing sources and build the wisdom, one upon the other.

The Tarot of Oz

Created by David Sexton

- 78 full-color cards and a 192-page mini-book in a slipcase

- Cards are 4⅝ x 3¼. with nonreversible backs and illustrated pips

- Based on L. Frank Baum's *The Wonderful World of Oz* series

- Full-color illustrations are inspired by the original artwork for the Oz series by John R. Neill, the "Royal Illustrator of Oz"

- Deck and book contain original spreads created specifically for the *Tarot of Oz*

- Merges the archetypes of the tarot with the characters and events of Oz, following Dorothy's travels on the Yellow Brick Road as she reenacts the Fool's Journey

2. ~ The Priestess
Glinda the Good

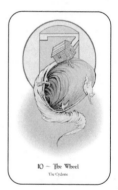

10 ~ The Wheel
The Cyclone

Seven ~ Swords

Queen ~ Wands
Erma, Queen of Light

Ten ~ Stones

Walking the Labyrinth

by James Wells

In the tarot community, there is a positive trend towards living out or acting upon a reading, rather than treating it as mere information. Since the early 1990s, walking the labyrinth has become a popular mode of healing and self-awareness. In this article, we will explore various ways to combine the two. What better way to embody your tarot insights than to employ the body itself?

"Labyrinth" is composed of two parts: the *labrys*, or double-headed axe, is an ancient symbol of the Goddess; "rinth" refers to a dwelling. So "labyrinth" means "house of the double-headed axe" or "home of the Goddess." This ancient pattern has been found in several cultures, including Crete, France, the American Southwest, and Great Britain.

A labyrinth is often circular—a universal symbol of wholeness, unity, and the eternal. It contains a single, if meandering, path upon which one walks from the periphery into the center and back again—a metaphor for our journey, whether internal or external. Those whose walking abilities are challenged can trace the pattern on a page with their fingers.

Labyrinths can have different numbers of circuits or revolutions around their centers, created by connecting a series of dots and lines called a seed pattern. There is a prevalence of three-, seven-, and eleven-circuit labyrinths, although others exist. Path outlines can be of any material—stones, reflective tape, ink, bricks, sidewalk chalk, sand, or shrubbery.

Without suggesting that there is any conscious connection between the labyrinth and the structure of the tarot, one cannot help but notice parallels. To walk the spiral is to journey; tarot is often referred to as "the Fool's journey." A three-circuit labyrinth can be likened to three rows of seven trumps (I–VII, VIII–XIV, and XV–XXI) with the center as zero, the Fool. A five-circuit labyrinth mirrors the four suits plus the Major Arcana, or the four court characters plus the Ace. Seven circuits embody seven groups of three trumps as well as those trumps which, in the Golden Dawn system, correspond with the seven inner or ancient planets. Eleven-circuit labyrinths can reflect eleven pairs of trumps.

Exploring the Labyrinth

Let's now explore how to combine the two tools in practice.

Prior to a tarot reading, walk the labyrinth to ground yourself, clarify your intent and questions, and enter an oracular mindset. Similarly, a labyrinth journey after a tarot session can help you to reflect on images, patterns, and information, to absorb it, and to

prepare you to re-enter mundania. A variation is to perform the tarot reading in the center of the labyrinth, sandwiched between entering and leaving.

Many people consecrate their labyrinths to a specific purpose or to an aspect of deity. You can ask your labyrinth, via the tarot, to whom or to what it would like to be dedicated. Sit beside or inside the circle, cards in hand. See or imagine an energetic connection between you and the meandering path. Gently mix your deck. Pick a single card to show you the labyrinth's affiliation. For example, the High Priestess might indicate that the labyrinth is dedicated to Isis or to divination. The Hanged Man could signify that Jesus, Odin, or the concept of surrender are connected to the spiral. The Sun may tell you to approach the labyrinth playfully or that Ra is the preferred deity.

Another way to use a single card is to pick one before a labyrinth walk to provide you with a theme to meditate on that day. Either leave it outside or carry it with you. Three cards may be employed— the first chosen beforehand for what you take into the labyrinth (or what you shed as you go in), the second chosen in the center for what you discover in the core that you will take back with you, and the third afterward for a concrete action to perform in the tangible world. I've also drawn five cards: beginning, journey in, center, journey out, and completion.

A Deeper Understanding

There are times when we need a richer understanding of a tarot card, either as part of an ongoing program of study or as a means to dig deeper into a challenging card from a reading. It helps to "enter into" such a tarot image through active imagination, most often accomplished while sitting in one spot in a state of contemplation. To involve the body in this process is to take it deeper, to imbibe and live out the card's energy. After contemplating your card, take it with you into the labyrinth knowing that as you traverse the winding path you are strolling through the tarot landscape, interacting directly with its symbols and characters. Make notes after your walk or carry a small cassette recorder as you journey. Vary this by placing a large color copy of the card in the center of the labyrinth, perhaps alongside or underneath a crystal sphere, mirror, or bowl of water so that you can enter even more profoundly into your card through scrying. Another creative variation is to ask people to be aspects of the tarot card and to stand in designated sections of the labyrinth. As you walk the path, you encounter each tarot symbol, action, and character through the words and actions of your friends. To enhance this experience even more, incorporate props, body paint, masks, costumes, scent, or music. By the end of this walk, you will know the card.

This sort of exciting interactive tarot ritual drama can also be employed to journey through a full spread. Each person is a card from the layout and, in a manner of speaking, "channels" the card's information to you during the course of the labyrinth walk. You may want one person to help sum up the entire living spread for you at the end. Once again, use as many, or as few, props as you wish.

Those who practice Western magic may want to partner the labyrinth with Qabalistic pathworking. In pathworking, the magus travels the paths on the Tree of Life with a specific intent to perform a working in a specific sephirah that corresponds with that intent. Each path corresponds with a Major Arcana card. To walk that path, the practitioner enters the card (see above) and journeys in the astral planes. Sometimes people enact this journey ritually, which is where the labyrinth comes in. Prepare for your pathworking. Set an intent and know which sephirah is best for that intent. Research archangels, god-names, colors, planets, etc. which link up with each of the sephiroth and pathways you must traverse in order to reach that specific sephirah. Discover which trumps go with which paths and which pips and/or courts go with which sephiroth. Any good book on magic will provide this information. In the center of your labyrinth, create an altar that resonates with your intent and with the sephirah you are using. Along the path, lay out the trumps that represent the paths you will walk on the

Tree of Life as well as pips to represent each sphere or station. Enter into each card in order as you walk the labyrinth and observe all that you experience on the inner planes. When you reach the center, your chosen sephirah, take time to acclimatize yourself to the environment, then perform your ritual. Reverse the process, then make copious notes on everything that happened.

Let me provide you with an example from my own experience. These are only the bare bones; specific details would take far too long to describe. My intent was to request that world leaders find creative and peaceable solutions to end war. The sephirah for that is Tipharet, in the center of the Qabalistic Tree. The two paths I needed to journey to get there correspond with the Universe/World and Temperance, so I placed trump XXI at the entrance to the labyrinth and number XIV about halfway through, just after the Minor Arcana Nines (I would need to make a sort of "rest stop" at the ninth sephirah on the way). On the altar in the center, I placed the four Sixes and the four Princes, as well as a picture of the United Nations flag and a thurible in which to burn frankincense. The landscapes for my walk into and out of the labyrinth were provided by the scenes on the cards. My prayers and energy projection in the center were enhanced by the presence of the tarot characters. It was a powerful and humbling experience.

Walking the Labyrinth

A truly enjoyable and liberating way to combine tarot and labyrinth together is to dance a tarot reading. Consult the cards as normal. Notice the poses the characters make and the actions that they carry out. Write down the poses and movements in order as they appear in the layout. Try out, with your body, this sequence of moves. When it feels "right," you have completed your choreography. Go to the labyrinth, turn on appropriate music, and dance your sequence of tarot movements all the way to the center and back. Don't worry about what it might mean, just do it! How do you feel now? What insights, if any, did you receive as you danced? Or was it all about sheer soul expression? Because I don't believe that humans are victims of fate, I sometimes break tarot "rules" by switching around the order of cards in a spread so that other options can present themselves to me—a game of "what if." If you decide to play with this idea, reflect it in your labyrinth dance by changing the order of your steps and poses. How is it different? Is it easier, more problematic, or the same for you to move in this new way? Dance yet another sequence, then another. This technique can help you to discover, by trying them on, which possibilities are perfect for you with regard to the subject of your reading. As before, you can call upon your friends (they'll either grow accustomed to these requests or run for cover). Each person dances through the labyrinth as a particular card from your layout. Note how these living, dancing pasteboards interact with one another. Are they cooperative? Does there seem to be conflict? Is it a graceful performance or does it need more polish? These are all further food for thought.

Use the number of circuits in your labyrinth to explore a spread with that number of layout positions. Walk a three-circuit labyrinth in order to delve into a past-present-possible futures reading or a body-mind-spirit spread. After casting a seven-card chakra assessment layout, journey through a seven-circuit labyrinth to integrate the reading, align the chakras, and begin the healing suggested in the reading. Those people who use a significator or a helper card as part of the Celtic Cross could gain more insight by travelling through an eleven-circuit labyrinth.

Poetry and affirmations are great ways to express tarot concepts succinctly. In a three-circuit labyrinth you could recite a haiku, which has three lines, as a mantra while journeying—one line of text per circuit. Or declare an affirmation you create from a tarot reading, either while walking or in the center.

Mix and match any of the aforementioned techniques to create an even richer experience for yourself. Perhaps your group does a tarot reading to discover the most appropriate way to celebrate the Autumnal Equinox in the labyrinth. From the cards you derive an appropriate intent, costume ideas, gestures, and so forth. Or maybe you write a series of poems based on tarot cards, set them to music, and sing them in a candlelit labyrinth.

There are as many ways to combine tarot and labyrinth as there are ideas in the world. May you never exhaust the possibilities!

A Mabon Tarot Ritual

by Nina Lee Braden

T he Pagan sabbat of Mabon takes place at the Fall Equinox. Each year, we have two days where day and night are equal: Spring and Fall Equinox. Spring Equinox, called in many Pagan calendars Ostara, heralds the half of the year when the Sun (or day) has dominance. Mabon, the Fall Equinox, heralds the yearly dominance of the Moon (or night). Mabon is also the second harvest. In this way, it is very much a day of thanksgiving and rejoicing, even as it ushers in the dark half of the year.

Although this ritual celebrates a Pagan holiday, it can be performed by people who are not Pagan. Anyone who uses the tarot and who wishes to celebrate the energies of the Fall Equinox and second harvest can find this ritual a wonderful celebration.

Preparing Your Space

This ritual is written to be done alone, but you can easily adapt it for working with a small or large group. Before beginning the ritual, you will need to set up a sacred space. Designate an area to be your working circle and have a small table to serve as an altar.

If you have at least two tarot decks, you can choose two decks to use in this ritual. If you only have one tarot deck, you will need to do a bit of advance work. Before beginning the ritual, go through one of

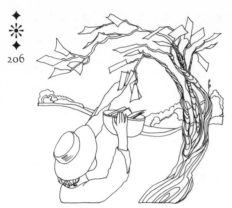

your tarot decks (or your only deck) and, with careful and devoted intent, choose, faceup, a card that most represents for you the blessings of air. Choose likewise a card for the blessings of fire, the blessings of water, and the blessings of earth. These cards do not need to be the purest representations of the elements but rather the blessings of the elements. Put these four cards on your altar.

A common altar placement is east/air, south/fire, west/water, and north/earth. Feel free to use these placements or whatever association you are accustomed to using. When you have done this, go through your deck faceup again, and choose two cards that represent to you a perfect balance between light and dark, Sun and Moon, white and black, or yang and yin. In addition, choose one card that represents for you the concept of harvest and another card for thanksgiving. Place these four cards in the center of your altar. Have your second tarot deck on the altar, ready for use.

If you only have one tarot deck, then you will need to substitute something for the cards you have chosen. You may make a photocopy of your cards, or you may draw or trace simple cards to use. The important thing is to have visual representations of the cards on the altar and also to have a complete deck available for divination. When you have put your copies or drawings on your altar, also place your complete deck on the altar.

Feel free to add anything else to your altar that you may wish, such as candles, incense, a bell, a statue, or a chalice of water. For Mabon, you may wish to have something representing the harvest or the balance of light and dark. The important thing is to make sure that you have room for all eight of the tarot cards that you have chosen, and room for your deck. If you are using a small table, you may only have room for the eight cards and your deck.

Before beginning the ritual, symbolically purify yourself in some way. Some people like to take a ritual bath or to ritually wash their hands. Other people like to smudge themselves with sage. Some people like to visualize themselves being bathed in a cone of light. Other people like to visualize themselves walking through a doorway of flames. For Mabon, you might want to ritually wash your hands in dry cornmeal. Once you have symbolically purified yourself, you are ready to begin your Mabon Tarot Ritual.

Performing the Ritual

Standing a few feet back from your altar, extend your dominant hand (the right hand, for most people). Using your index finger, draw a circle around your altar and around yourself. Imagine that a beam of light extends from your finger. You are establishing sacred space. Taking a cleansing breath, step up to your altar.

Holding up the card that you have chosen to represent the blessings of air, say: "By [name of card], I give thanks to the element of air for all of the many blessings that I have received during the past six months. I thank the element of air for the breath in my lungs, for the songs in my ears, and for the voice in my throat. I thank the air for the sweet breezes that bring to me the perfume of the honeysuckle, the aroma of the grasses, and the song of the bird. So mote it be."

Holding up the card that you have chosen to represent the blessings of fire, say: "By [name of card], I give thanks to the element of fire for all of the many blessings that I have received during the past six months. I thank the element of fire for the heat of my body, and for the warmth in the smiles, handshakes, and hugs of others. I thank the element of fire for the light and warmth of the Sun, and for the gift of fire—from which so many other gifts spring. So mote it be."

Holding up the card that you have chosen to represent the blessings of water, say: "By [name of card], I give thanks to the element of water for all of the many blessings that I have received during the past six months. I thank the element of water for the blood and other fluids that course through my body. I thank the element of water for the raindrops that fall, for the rivers and streams that flow through my neighborhood, and the vast seas and oceans that birthed life on our planet. So mote it be."

Holding up the card that you have chosen to represent the blessings of earth, say: "By [name of card], I give thanks to the element of earth for all of the many blessings that I have received during the past six months. I thank the element of earth for my teeth and my bones, which give form and substance to my body and which are my shield and strength. I thank the element of earth for the vast deserts and plains, for the rocks of the mountains, and for the fertile soil and the plants that grow in that soil. So mote it be."

Raise your hands over your head and say, "I come today to celebrate life and its abundance. I celebrate the second harvest. I celebrate the fruits of the harvest. I celebrate the toil of those who planted and the toil of those who reaped. I give thanks to earth, water, fire, and air for aiding in the growth of this harvest. I give thanks to Divine Spirit, which nurtures me not only physically but emotionally, mentally, and spiritually. I give thanks for all gifts, for I am indeed blessed."

At this point, pick up the two cards that represent harvest and thanksgiving. Look carefully at the cards. Try to mentally blend the two cards so that they represent one extended scene, a space where one card merges into the other card. Using this landscape as your background, and holding one card in each hand, say, "I dance the spiral dance in the landscape of harvest and thanksgiving." Then, still with the cards in your hands and staying within your sacred space, do a small spiral dance. Normally, we dance clockwise, but feel free to move as you are inspired. Dance with thanksgiving and celebration. Dance to the rhythm of your heartbeat. Dance in honor of the harvest. Dance with your heart, mind, and soul. Picture yourself in your tarot landscape as you dance.

When you are done with your dance, place your cards back on your altar. Pick up the two remaining cards, the cards representing balance. Holding one in each hand, say, "I come today asking for a special message. Today is one of two days of equal balance. Today is a day when the Sun and Moon have equal reign, when day and

night are in perfect balance of power. Today, male perfectly balances female, and female perfectly balances male. Today, expansion balances restriction, and restriction balances expansion. Today, hot balances cold, and wet balances dry. Today, mercy balances severity. Today is the day of the middle way."

Place your two cards of balance back on the altar. Pick up your deck of tarot cards. "Today, I come asking for a divination. Today, I come asking for a message. I ask for a message of balance, a message of healing. I come asking for a personal message, but I come asking for a message for the world. I come asking for a message by which I can find balance in my own life for the next six months. I come asking for a message that I can share with others seeking balance in the next six months. On this day of perfect balance, I seek a message empowering me in my personal search for balance but also a message to help my troubled world find balance. So mote it be."

Shuffle your deck, concentrating on your intent. If you have a special spread that you want to use, feel free to use it. Otherwise, here is a simple one that you can use:

Card 1: My card of personal power for the next six months

Card 2: My card of my spiritual enlightenment for the next six months

Card 3: How I may best find personal balance during the next six months

Card 4: How I may best help the planet find balance during the next six months

Lay the cards out in a simple square or box. What is your message from the cards? How can your live it in your life for the next six months?

At this point, make a ritual gesture of thanksgiving—thanksgiving for the message of the cards, thanksgiving for the balance of the day, thanksgiving for the harvest, and thanksgiving for the gift of life. Your gesture may be simple, or it may be elaborate. You may wish to utter words of thanksgiving such as these:

"O Divine Spirit, thank you for the message of balance which you have given to me through the tarot. I will hold this message in my heart and nurture it so that I may grow in harmony and wisdom. I will use my mouth and hands and feet to make this message manifest in my own life. I will strive to live this message daily and thereby bless not only myself but others. Blessed be the inspiration, and blessed be the Divine Inspirer."

Picking up the card that represents the blessings of earth, say: "By [name of card], I give thanks to the element of earth for aiding me in my divination. I will strive to live the message of balance this year in order to bless the element of earth and to help in the healing of the Earth."

Picking up the card that represents the blessings of water, say: "By [name of card], I give thanks to the element of water for aiding me in my divination. I will strive to live the message of balance this year in order to bless the element of water and to help in the healing of the oceans, rivers, and other bodies of water."

Picking up the card that represents the blessings of fire, say: "By [name of card], I give thanks to the element of fire for aiding me in my divination. I will strive to live the message of balance this year in order to bless the element of fire and to help in the conservation of fuels and other forms of energy."

Picking up the card that represents the blessings of air, say: "By [name of card], I give thanks to the element of air for aiding me in my divination. I will strive to live the message of balance this year in order to bless the element of air and to help in the purification of the atmosphere so that all may have clean air to breathe."

Exit your sacred space and ground yourself by eating a snack, taking a ritual bath, sitting quietly and holding a crystal, or by shuffling your deck of tarot cards and then placing them in their resting order.

Working Without Cards

by Janina Renée

I sometimes get letters from prison inmates who have a copy of one of my books on tarot interpretation but are unable to get a pack of tarot cards. (In some prisons, they are allowed to have books but are not permitted to have cards.) No doubt there are other persons beside prisoners who are interested in the tarot, but unable to obtain cards because they are costly or otherwise unobtainable. In such cases, I advise them that they can still make use of my book, or any book on tarot, (or any book at all). Here are some things that anyone can do:

Bibliomancy

There is an ancient form of divination known as *bibliomancy* (the Greek word *biblios* means "book"). You can use any book for this, including a dictionary, telephone book, or novel—or, indeed, a Bible. To try this technique, pose a question in a meditative or prayerful way, then take a book and flip it open, with the idea that whichever page you get will have some meaningful message for your situation. Some practitioners take this a step further by opening the book and, with their eyes closed, putting a finger down on the page, with the idea that whatever sentence the finger lands on will be relevant to the question. In the case of a tarot book, you could do an entire tarot spread with bibliomancy. For example, if you want to do a five-card spread, just ask your question, concentrating on it for a few seconds in your mind. Whichever tarot card is represented on the first page you open will be your first card. Close the book, concentrate, and open the book a second time, and whichever card is shown will be your second card—and so on until you've finished the spread.

Meditation

If your book has relatively decent illustrations, you can meditate on the tarot images. Just gaze at one of the pictures, then close your eyes and hold it in your mind. Try to hold the card in mind for as long as possible, and see if any interesting insights or impressions pop up. You can do this even before you read the interpretations for a given card.

Freewriting

Using the illustrations, you can also generate inspiration through "freewriting." Just choose a card illustration, concentrate on it for a few seconds, and then write down everything that pops into your mind. Try to write continuously, in a stream of consciousness, without laying down your pen until you have filled a certain number of pages or minutes. You may be surprised by the personal insights that emerge.

Deep Description

Also using card illustrations, you can gain new insight through the "deep description" technique. As described in my book, *Tarot for a New Generation*, you "write down everything you see in the card, noticing things like the colors used, incidental objects in the background or foreground, whether or not there is a border, what kind of lettering is used if there is a label, whether any of the objects or arrangements of objects form geometrical shapes, whether any of the human figures look out at you, what sort of gestures they are making, and much more." This is more difficult than it may sound, because you must include only what you see, and not what you think or feel about any of the images. If you can stick to the discipline and not form any opinions until afterward, new revelations will arise.

Visualization

You can use tarot images for visualization exercises to help you with common needs. For example, to work toward greater calm in the midst of a chaotic environment, visualize yourself achieving the serene consciousness of the High Priestess. If you feel you need greater competence in the art of verbal self-defense, picture yourself modeling the alertness and quick-though-situationally-appropriate responses of the King or Queen of Swords.

Dream Interpretation

You can use the book for dream interpretation if you have any dreams with images that can be correlated with tarot images. Thus, if you dream of an old man, this might relate to card IX, the Hermit, and if you dream of a lion, this might relate to card VIII, Strength.

Using an Alternate Deck

If you have a pack of ordinary playing cards, you can divine by interpreting the Hearts as Cups, the Diamonds as Pentacles, the Clubs as Wands, and the Spades as Swords. The Knaves can combine the meanings of the Knights and Pages, showing communications and active involvement. The Joker can represent the Fool, or you could use him to denote a situation in flux, where events may take a number of different directions. Although this lacks the philosophical dimension that the other Major Arcana cards would bring to a reading, it still enables you to explore many different areas of life.

Giving from the Heart

by Valerie Sim

When it comes to gift-giving, I admit to being terribly opinionated. And I especially abhor the commercialism of Christmas. I have gone through many spiritual changes, but this revulsion has remained constant, no matter my path or its label. Don't get me wrong: I love to give gifts . . . when I want to. But I hate gift-giving on demand. I think this is the reason I begin working on my gift ideas months before the holiday or occasion they will commemorate. It's not that I am exceedingly practical—it is just the only way, within my budget, I can get/make whatever I want for everyone dear to me, rather than just coughing up "something" because the occasion dictates and wrapping it in pretty, soon-to-be-shredded paper.

It was musing along these lines that made me realize that most of the gifts I have most cherished have not arrived during the holidays, and for those of you waiting for me to get to the point: these gifts were tarot cards. No, not decks of cards; cards made for me personally or inspired in some way by me and given with love and a smile.

The first time I was gifted with a card, I was utterly shocked and uncharacteristically speechless. Ellen Lorenzi-Prince was the first person who ever "gave" me a card—in the sense that she dedicated

The Six of Wands from the *Tarot of the Crone*

her Six of Wands from her *Tarot of the Crone* to me. When I first looked at this card I got goosebumps. Never before had someone about whom I cared linked me to a creation from her heart. As I "read" this card, I almost cried.

The *Tarot of the Crone* is about each person's inner process. This particular card is about living in tune with the beat of your own drummer even when you feel it is a song that others may not hear, or might not like, and knowing that that doesn't matter. What matters is that you love the song, that it comes genuinely from your own heart, and that you sing it freely from a sense of internal harmony. Amazingly, when you do this you often find others singing along with you. It is truly a radiant moment.

This card will always be an inspiration to me, and when I pull it when using this deck I always feel that original thrill, and know that no matter what my doubts are, or how heavy my burden seems at the time, all I have to do is to stop, listen for that song so dear to me, and get back on my path. Thank you, Ellen!

The second time I was gifted with a card, it was completely different. Lorena Moore tells me she was already painting the card for her *Ironwing Tarot* (in progress) when my energy inserted itself into her consciousness. I know this sounds a bit invasive, but I don't think Lorena felt it to be that way at all. This was not meant to be "my card," nor is it actually "mine." But Lorena told me that as she painted, she "felt" me, and that connection influenced her art. What emerged on her canvas was indeed an accurate energy picture of my journey

The Eight of Spikes from the *Ironwing Tarot*

at that time and she knew it instantly and intuitively.

I am still staggered that she painted a phoenix and his fiery flight at the very time I was working to rebirth something very important to me that had almost been consumed. And notice that the body of the great bird is a flute! Even in the heat of the contest it was only my "music" that kept me on track. The truly incredible thing about this story (skip this if you are not a believer in synchronicity) is that as I struggled to write down my instantaneous poetic reaction to her image and reply to her e-mail, I heard

217

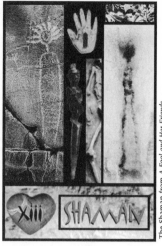

The Shaman from *A Fool and Her Friends*

a strange noise and turned around. Somehow, miraculously, a bird had managed to fly beyond the lethal blades of my whole house fan and emerge live and flapping into my living room. I can't tell you how I felt as I went on autopilot to get my cats out of the room so that I could usher that modern-day phoenix outside to freedom. And that bird did fly free, with me watching in complete awe and wonder . . . lesson not lost . . . Lorena, you sustained me!

A few months ago, I received a third gift, totally different from the previous two, but every bit as meaningful. My friend Sally Anne Stephen has many talents. Lately she has discovered that those talents extend to tarot art, and she conceived of creating a deck of Majors, each inspired by a different tarot friend of hers, which she calls *A Fool and Her Friends*.

When I saw my card, I trembled and thrilled. Yes! Someone truly understood what it is I feel called to do on this shamanic journey of mine. I am a shamanic deathwalker, who, much like the midwife, helps make a life-passage more comfortable—both for those making that journey and for the ones they love. This card, while remaining true to the Death archetype, captures my personal journey, the timeliness/timelessness, the fact that we are all connected and should always remain so. Sally Anne, you are a genius.

I can't tell you how much these gifts have meant to me. They were not given as a result of any expectation. None were "necessary." They were all given from the heart and as per the talents of each soul's personal creativity. Each is utterly priceless.

So, though I realize not everyone has the artistic urge or inspiration to start creating tarot cards for those they love, I encourage you to let this little article inspire you to give of yourself in a truly personal way, no mall necessary. What can you make or do for someone you love that is special? Not all of us are artists. Some write poetry. Some do crafts. Some bake. The possibilities are nearly endless.

May all holidays and special occasions be joyous and meaningful to all of you, no matter your personal spiritual connections, and may all your gifts, both those given and received, be truly from the heart.

Business Cards

by Mark McElroy

Quick: name the four most important tools a businessperson can carry. A laptop, perhaps? Great idea. A Palm Pilot? Absolutely. A cell phone? Of course.

And tarot cards?

Wait—tarot cards? Those seventy-eight pieces of laminated cardboard Sister Doololly uses to tell fortunes? Why in the world would a businessperson want to carry tarot cards?

What if I told you that, with tarot cards, you can generate twenty-two practical ideas for making more money, working more efficiently, or advancing your career? What if you could generate those ideas in less than twenty minutes? And what if carrying a tarot deck meant you could tap into this creative wellspring anytime, anywhere, as often as you liked?

Suddenly, carrying tarot cards in your briefcase makes a lot more sense.

Bear in mind, though, that using tarot cards to boost your career or affect the bottom line requires us to move beyond using tarot as a fortunetelling prop. We have to start seeing tarot cards as business cards.

Creativity Equals Cash

It's just a fact: creativity makes good business sense. Innovating a new product? Investigating why sales are down? Creating a dazzling marketing campaign? Outwitting the competition? Coming up with reasons why you should be manager—or even CEO? Every single one of these enterprises requires creativity . . . and lots of it!

But as someone who spent almost a decade laboring for one of the planet's largest telecommunications companies, I can tell you this with authority: in the business world, creativity is in short supply. The same ideas get recycled again and again. Despite the fact that last year's strategies proved ineffective, they're dressed up and paraded around as this year's new vision.

And corporations aren't the only ones suffering from a creativity deficit. Small businesses owners, trying to stay afloat, are frequently too busy or too tired to pursue creative solutions. Employees at every level, rushing to meet today's deadlines, rarely have time to think of tomorrow. They've barely got a moment to snatch a gulp of water from the cooler, let alone come up with strategies that, if implemented today, might make tomorrow more profitable for both themselves and their companies.

And that's where a tarot deck comes in handy. Using a tarot deck—in fact, just using the trumps from a tarot deck—can help the busiest of people generate twenty-two fantastic business solutions in less than twenty minutes.

Imagine it: twenty-two new product ideas. Twenty-two insights into declining sales—and how to perk them up again. Twenty-two ideas for your ad campaign. Twenty-two ways to slaughter the competition. Twenty-two strategies for advancing your career.

What Would the Trumps Do?

The process, called "What Would the Trumps Do?" (or WWTD for short), invites you to explore your question, see your situation, and plan action from twenty-two points of view—those of the tarot trump cards. After defining your need, you present your problem to each member of the Major Arcana, asking, "So what would you do in my situation?" While keeping the unique perspective of the trump in mind, you jot down the first answer that pops into your head—no matter how outrageous, bizarre, elaborate, or mundane it may be.

If you're more familiar with balancing the books than you are with tarot cards, the handy list that follows suggests a perspective to associate with each trump.

The Trumps: Keywords and Possibilities

0—Fool
Enthusiasm, Inexperience, Playfulness, Trickiness
. . . a total beginner . . .
. . . a practical joker . . .
. . . a young upstart . . .
. . . someone wanting to impress the boss . . .
. . . someone just having fun . . .

1—Magician
Empowerment, Creativity, Awareness, Skill
. . . an action hero . . .
. . . a person with magical powers . . .
. . . someone in charge . . .
. . . a "do it yourself" person . . .
. . . a "whiz kid" . . .

2—Priestess
Reflection, Reception, Secrecy, Analysis
. . . an analyst . . .
. . . a psychic . . .
. . . a wise woman . . .
. . . someone "behind the scenes" . . .
. . . someone with a hidden agenda . . .

3—Empress
Development, Growth, Nurturing, Productivity
. . . my mother . . .
. . . an expert coach . . .
. . . a productivity expert . . .
. . . an environmentalist . . .
. . . a nurturing mentor . . .

4—Emperor
Authority, Directives, Order, Organization, Control
. . . my father . . .
. . . someone with rigid opinions . . .
. . . The boss or the CEO . . .
. . . a "take control" person . . .
. . . someone who delegates everything . . .

The Trumps: Keywords and Possibilities

5—Hierophant
Externals, Regulations, Appearances, Standards
. . . a "by the book" person . . .
. . . someone wanting to look good . . .
. . . an expensive consultant . . .
. . . a "goody-two-shoes" . . .
. . . a PR person . . .

6—Lovers
Affiliations, Partnerships, Networking, Team Spirit
. . . a good team player . . .
. . . a great business partner . . .
. . . my best friend . . .
. . . a terrific vendor . . .
. . . a group of friends . . .

7—Chariot
Victories, Triumphs, Competition, Excellence
. . . the "Employee of the Year" . . .
. . . an undefeated quarterback . . .
. . . a "take no prisoners" competitor . . .
. . . my role model . . .
. . . a ruthless military commander . . .

8—Strength
Resolve, Focus, Dependability, Reserve
. . . Superman . . .
. . . someone who thinks physically . . .
. . . a "take action now" person . . .
. . . a reliable, trusted worker . . .
. . . a confident manager . . .

9—Hermit
Solitude, Isolation, Time, Experience
. . . someone with unlimited time . . .
. . . a spiritual leader . . .
. . . a wise old man . . .
. . . a seasoned worker . . .
. . . a one-person shop . . .

The Trumps: Keywords and Possibilities

10—Wheel
Cycles, Fluctuations, Luck, Fate
. . . someone in tune with trends . . .
. . . the previous manager or CEO . . .
. . . someone taking a random approach . . .
. . . a "best case/worst case" person . . .
. . . someone motivated by habit . . .

11—Justice
Evaluations, Deliberations, Objectivity, Fairness
. . . a lawyer . . .
. . . someone known for fairness . . .
. . . King Solomon . . .
. . . Mr. Spock . . .
. . . someone honest to a fault . . .

12—Hanged Man
Trial, Transformation, Traitors, Hard Knocks
. . . the competition . . .
. . . someone about to leave the company . . .
. . . someone making a mistake . . .
. . . someone experiencing déjà-vu . . .
. . . a person who shakes things up . . .

13—Death
Endings, Transitions, Finality, Conclusion
. . . someone determined to end this . . .
. . . someone wanting to be fired . . .
. . . someone with nothing to lose . . .
. . . someone wanting to get on with it . . .
. . . someone with a fatalistic attitude . . .

14—Temperance
Blending, Mediation, Averaging, Combining
. . . an arbitration expert . . .
. . . someone "middle of the road" . . .
. . . a politically correct person . . .
. . . someone who values "getting along" . . .
. . . an average joe . . .

The Trumps: Keywords and Possibilities

15—Devil
Manipulation, Callousness, Materialism, Profit
. . . someone who values profit over all . . .
. . . Machiavelli . . .
. . . a "get rich quick" person . . .
. . . a manipulative person . . .
. . . a deceptive person . . .

16—Tower
Destruction, Revision, Breakage, Failure
. . . a pessimist . . .
. . . a "tear it down, start over" person . . .
. . . a person new to this situation . . .
. . . a destructive person . . .
. . . a demolition expert . . .

17—Star
Hope, Goals, Dreams, Beauty
. . . an actor or actress . . .
. . . an optimist . . .
. . . a performance coach . . .
. . . a person focused on the future . . .
. . . a dreamer . . .

18—Moon
Illogic, Inversion, Madness, Romance
. . . a person doing the wrong thing . . .
. . . a certifiably crazy person . . .
. . . a wild man . . .
. . . a trailblazer . . .
. . . a risk-taker . . .

19—Sun
Celebrations, Satisfaction, Achievement, Appreciation
. . . a person seeking recognition . . .
. . . a person intent on winning . . .
. . . the best employee at the company . . .
. . . a happy person . . .
. . . the brightest person I know . . .

The Trumps: Keywords and Possibilities

20—Judgment
Decisions, Conclusions, Opportunity, Reality
. . . a person with unlimited authority . . .
. . . a historian looking back on this . . .
. . . a general rallying the troops . . .
. . . a person with the one right answer . . .
. . . a decisive person . . .

21—World
Completion, Realization, Fullness, Joy
. . . a "tie up loose ends" person . . .
. . . a person who has it all . . .
. . . a person with no financial limits . . .
. . . a person with no limits at all . . .
. . . someone with no agenda . . .

Here's an example of how the process works: a corporate think-tank sits down to brainstorm answers to the question, "How can we boost our sagging sales?" Using the WWTD process, they generate the following list in under twenty minutes. In each case, it's easy to see how their ideas for action relate to the perspective of the associated trump.

- Fool: Study how the company began, so we can copy our own early success

- Magician: Verify that what's going on above (management) is understood below (employees)

- Priestess: Survey the employee population to capture "productivity secrets" that might change how we're doing business

- Empress: Foster growth by linking pay to productivity and company numbers

- Emperor: Have managers observe workers more closely and learn to give better direction

- Hierophant: Bring in motivational speakers

- Lovers: Show appreciation for top performing groups with days off, money, etc.

- Chariot: Have a sales competition keyed to corporate goals or asking for ideas

- Strength: Define what we do best, then find out how we're departing from that

- Hermit: Sponsor a retreat focused on articulating a clear business plan at every company level

- Wheel: Determine whether this downturn is a symptom of a larger cycle—and investigate how the company survived similar cycles in the past

- Justice: Define the rules that constrain how business is done—and try breaking them

- Hanged Man: Turn the system upside down by working backward from our goals to define what we must do (and when we must do it) to achieve them

- Death: Discover what out-of-date systems or policies need to go

- Temperance: Eliminate boundaries between senior management and employees, making direct contact possible

- Devil: Realize that cutting costs isn't the only way we can affect the bottom line

- Tower: Start from scratch; level the organizational chart and build it over again

- Star: Define clear goals for the year

- Moon: Remind ourselves of why we love working here, the spirit that brought us here, and the dreams we make possible

- Sun: Celebrate past victories and build a culture of success by sharing the stories

- Judgment: Make people more directly accountable for their actions by measuring performance more objectively

- World: Think beyond this crisis. When we solve it, where do we go?

Putting just one of these ideas into motion could make a real and measurable difference in the company's bottom line. Best of all, instead of spending $22,000 to bring in a consultant for the day, they've captured the input of twenty-two consultants—for the price of one tarot deck.

Putting the Tarot to Work

Armed with the "What Would the Trumps Do?" strategy, you're ready to start meeting your own business challenges and tap into the unlimited creative energy of the tarot trumps. Define your goal, turn off your inner critic (because even your nuttiest ideas may later give rise to powerful, practical insights), and brainstorm your way to greater business success.

Tarot of the Saints

Created and illustrated by Robert M. Place

- 78 full-color cards and a 248-page illustrated book

- Cards are 2¾ x 4¾, with nonreversible backs and illustrated pips

- Illustrations feature gold metallic ink on card borders and halos

- Explores medieval religious mysticism and its connection to tarot archetypes

- Explains the histories and legends of each saint featured in the deck and their places in the the tarot mythos

XV · ST. MARGARET AND THE DEVIL

EIGHT OF COINS

TWO OF CUPS

ST. ROCH · SQUIRE OF STAFFS

VIII · ST. MICHAEL · JUSTICE

Tarot Journaling

by Winter Wren

The word "journal" comes from the old French word *journée*, which means "a day." The original meaning of the word "journey" was the distance one could travel in one day, and a journal was the book that held a record of what happened in that day on that journey. The Major Arcana of the tarot are often referred to as the Fool's Journey or the Hero's Journey: you travel through the cards on your journey through life. A journal is both a journey in itself and the record of the journey taken. The journey to the new place, the new you, is both exciting and a thing of some fear. It is new. What waits ahead?

Beginning journal keepers and beginning tarotists often experience the same feelings. A new tarot deck brings the excitement of opening the package; the unique "new" smell of the deck; the rush of intensity with the artwork on each card; the appreciation of the smooth, perfect edges. With the new journal comes the sheer joy of the lovely cover, the amazement at the crisp, clean pages. The deck and the book are new, bright, unmarred, perfect. They are too perfect. How can you use them? And now comes the feeling of trepidation. The cards could become bent. You don't have the right kind of pen for the bright pages. The handwriting is not good enough for this treasured book. New can be gratifying, but it also keeps these things from becoming yours. These tools are only useful if you actually use them.

Individually, tarot and journaling are two strong tools for your personal journey of self-awareness and growth. Tarot and journaling each allow a new point of view about your life to enter your mind. Combined, these two tools complement and support each other in powerful and life-changing ways. It is a matter of removing old notions about rules from the mind and freeing yourself to think and grow in entirely new directions.

Anyone can use the tarot to further his or her spiritual and personal development: you do not have to be an experienced practitioner to access its insights. It is a medium that encourages development of your own inner potential, and provides a framework on which to structure the canvas while that new being is painted. The tarot provides each seeker with a vast array of symbolism leading to higher knowledge and consciousness, much of which is buried in the depths of the subconscious. The wonderful variety of tarot decks available today offers a previously unequaled quantity of traditions, styles, and symbolism with which you may aid your growth. The tarot is most helpful to your spiritual growth and inner development when it is viewed as a key for opening the mind to greater awareness.

Self-development and coming to know the inner self are things not quickly or easily achieved. This process requires time as well as honesty and patience. This is not a journey to be undertaken lightly: it is likely to bring about internal conflict. Internal conflict may be difficult to deal with, but it is necessary to bring your inner self into focus. In our current society, it is rare that we allow ourselves much

time for introspection. We hold too little sacred in our world. We hold too little spiritual in our world. The sacred and the spiritual come from within, and the tarot is an excellent way to get back in touch with that part of ourselves. We tend to lose sight of the person we really are in our attempts to maintain standing and security. The tarot is a road back to you.

A journal is another tool of self-growth and understanding. It is one that goes hand in hand with the tarot. Like the tarot, a journal is an extension of you. It is an investment in self. It is a reason to pause in your day and reflect on not only the day, but on your thoughts and feelings. There is solace, peace, and knowledge to be found in writing and reflection. In your journal, your tarot work can intermingle with your life, with your feelings, with your remembered dreams—with you.

Starting Out

Many people have trouble with the concept of a journal or feel overwhelmed by the thought of keeping one. However, it is likely these feelings come because many view the journaling concept as "keeping a diary." Diaries are confining and often doomed to failure, very much in the same way as New Year's resolutions are. You are "supposed" to write in them every day, and so something of a guilt complex tends to build when you fall behind. As the guilt builds, so does the level of frustration—to the point that you end up discarding the whole idea.

A journal is a different matter entirely. Write in it as you do your tarot work or as something moves you to write in it. If that turns out to be every day, great! There are some who write in their journals more than once a day. But if you only work with your journal once a week, then so be it. Even then, you may have some days that feel so out of kilter that meditation, reflection, and writing are the only way to make sense of the day at hand. A journal is not about rules. Rules do not apply to journals. Neatness does not count. Grammar does not apply. Margins were made to be doodled in. It is okay to scratch out, but don't censor yourself. It is not important that you write well—it is important that you write. Set yourself free. Don't make journaling or tarot work a matter of a guilt response.

Just as you have choice in the realm of tarot decks, you have choice in the realm of journals. A journal can be kept in many ways: handwritten, on your computer, in cyberspace, or even on an audiotape. All have positives and negatives, so it is truly a matter of what is right for you. A hard-copy journal expands the possibilities in many ways. After all, a journal need not be a book of only words. Experiment with keeping your journal in colored pens. Try different colors of papers. Consider adhering miniature copies of the tarot cards for the day right on the journal pages. The same can be done with that feather or leaf found on your doorstep this morning that made you think differently of your day. Use stickers if you want. Add in that memorable fortune from the cookie at lunch. Let your journal reflect who you are.

When you settle in for a session of tarot journaling work, do so in a reverent and positive manner. The reverence is not so much for your tools, but for your own self. Be at peace with the world around you, at least for the time of your meditations. Let this be your place of reflection and a sacred time and space in your day. Time for self is a necessary component of sanity, and it is important to make that block of time something that you can anticipate eagerly. It is not selfish to set aside special time or even a special place—it is healthy to do so.

Create a space for yourself that you enjoy coming to each day. Make the space comfortable and inviting. Let it be your own little retreat. Have your tools ready at hand so you do not have to waste your special time hunting things that you need. Incense, background music, candles, a special pillow, or a pot of tea are some things that could add to the inviting ambiance of your area. Fill it with your beauty.

Writing It All Down

With the tools established, it is time to unite the travelers on the path. Start simply: choose one card from the deck—the card that calls most to you. Spend some time getting to know the card: what do you see in the card? What emotions do you find the card invoking within you? Write about them. Take the card apart in your mind. Write about individual parts of it. Does a figure in the card awaken a story in your mind? Write the story; give the figure life. Does the scene in the card dredge up a memory from your past? Write it down. Explore the how and the why. Create your own version of the card within your journal. Cut up magazines for pictures to glue into your journal creating your very own collage version of the card. Does it help you understand the card more? Does it change how you feel about the card? Write notes and feelings all around the card you created. Glue a thumbnail image of the original card on the page as well. Don't hold back; let the words flow. One note: do take the time to date your entries and, if writing multiple times in a day, consider including the time as well. It may seem tedious at the time, but you will thank yourself later as you see the record of how your thoughts evolved.

As your tarot journey pro-
gresses, let your journal
progress with it. Write about
the cards you draw for yourself each day. Put thumbnail
copies of the card into the
journal and note what the
positions stood for in your
daily spread. Go back later
and write about the events of
the day: how did the cards
reflect the happenings? Is
there something you view dif-

ferently about the cards now that the day is ending? do the cards
invite additional questions as much as they bring answers? Write
the questions and explore the answers.

As time passes, go back and read previous entries. Do not tear
out old pages or cross out old writing—rather, make notes about
new insights alongside the earlier writings. Use a different color
pen, if you want, to signify the new writings. Remember to add a
date to the new thoughts as well. Later, when reflecting on your
growth or seeking affirmation, that bit of information can provide
highly insightful to you. Write about patterns you see in your life
and then draw tarot cards for clarification about those patterns. If
you need to change a pattern, write about it, then draw a tarot
helper card to aid you in those changes. Write an affirmation of
positive change with your tarot assistant.

Putting It Into Practice

Use your journal to help you grow in your understanding of tarot
as well. Do not limit yourself to one tarot deck—explore new ones.
Investigate them just as deeply as you did your first one. Journal on
the differences you feel with the new cards. Let the unique colors,
symbolism, and artwork of this deck invoke a whole new awareness in you. Compare your favorite card from a previous deck to the
version of that card in the new deck: does it bring you new insights?
Does it awaken new memories? Write it all down. Go back and
reread what you wrote before. Perhaps you like the card better in
your new deck? Do you suddenly feel you are betraying a trusted
old friend? Let those thoughts flow onto your paper. Allow yourself
this growth. Allow your journey to continue.

In time, your pristine journal becomes battered, a bit dog-eared, perhaps not quite so clean. The book no longer closes well because of all the things pasted onto the pages. At last, the final page is filled. Place it on the shelf with your other treasured volumes. Pull it down once in while and read the steps you took to bring you to the place and person you are today.

Rainy-Day Tarot Projects

by *Thalassa*

Sooner or later you realize that the tarot is an endless source of stimulation. Working with the images and symbols often seems to generate a creative tizzy that is initially discovered in meditation, readings, and journaling, and works its way outward to manifest in the urge to explore artistic potential. Fevered by inspiration, many people make tarot-inspired artwork, versions of individual cards, or even create their own entire decks (a vapors-inducing task I will leave to more driven—and genuinely creative—spirits than my own). Some people paint, others write books. I cut the borders off of cards and play divination games with found objects. It's not da Vinci, but it makes me happy.

The following is my personal odyssey of how following the inspiration of the tarot led me to amuse and divert myself with decks of cards and an assortment of common household objects.

One could say decks were harmed (I prefer to take the A. E. Waite approach and say that I "rectified" them), and if there is a "People for the Ethical Treatment of Tarot Cards" out there, I apologize in advance and advise them to read another, less potentially trau-matic, article. For those plucky souls that remain, I hope that some readers will be inspired by my experiences. At the very least they may brighten up a boring day—they might even solve a case of tarot-block—but you will never look at card borders the same way.

That First Heady Sip

It all started with words. Blame it on the Golden Dawn. Working with the *Thoth* deck, I grew increasingly annoyed with Mr. Crowley's one-word pronouncements ceaselessly drawing my eye while I was trying to focus on the disturbingly beautiful images. Those images were already so rich in meaning, so much more eloquent than a single (often grim, stuffy, or judgmental) word could convey, that I felt I was fighting with the verbiage (after all, one cannot *not* read). And so it was that one fine day I decided to rob those mute pasteboards of their words, and I cut the troublesome borders off the cards. It was hard, at first—the first snip felt like I was defiling an art book (and I was certain I felt the gimlet eyes of Sister Mary St. Cyr, my grade-school's fiercely bibliophilic librarian, resting on me from beyond the grave). However, several deep breaths and a flourish of Fiskars later, I was stunned to see Frieda Harris's artwork in unbridled (or at least unbordered) splendor. The cards spoke more vividly than I could have imagined, and led me to discover new depths of meanings (many of which old uncle Aleister might not have cared about, but he's not here to fight me over them). Interestingly, bereft of their borders, the cards turned out to have small individual differences in size, making a deck of slight but pleasingly unstandardized heft. This pleased the anarchist aesthete in me and gave the experience a little tactile boost. My glow of triumph was somewhat mitigated when I later learned that I was far from a pioneer, that numerous folk—including no less august a tarotist than Mary Greer—had done the same thing to their *Thoth* decks. However, it was obscurely comforting to know that I was not a lone card mutilator. Thereafter, no deck was safe

The *Sacred Circle Tarot* was next (and I hope that the good folks at Llewellyn will not treat me too harshly for the manual abridgement of their fine product). An original and in some cases alternative interpretation of the deck (and refreshingly non-Qabalistic for those of us who like our Qabala on the side rather than tossed into our tarot salads), I admired it for its clever interlace of computer-generated and natural illustrations, as well as the Celtic-archetypal interpretation of traditional images (as was about to be revealed, this was most beautifully realized in the Major Arcana). Working with the deck, I found the stark white letters on the stark black background distracting (I will admit I found "Bondage" intriguing, but I digress). One sunny Sunday morning I found myself cackling maniacally while running through the house with scissors (in defiance of maternal childhood admonishments), and relieving another set of cards of its borders. When I was done the deck was like liquid magic in my hands. Without numbers or names on the Majors I was forced to pay attention strictly to the images and what they revealed. As an iconoclast who has never met an icon I didn't want to clast, I was still rather stunned at how freeing it was to let the cards talk directly to me in this fashion (which is just as well, since I could no longer remember which fabulous image corresponded to which Trump, and magical improvisation became the order of the day).

Cutting Loose

I have vanquished words from my card table. Since those heady early days with the Crowley and *Sacred Circle*, the constellation of decks I have surgically altered has grown to include the *Handl* and *Egyptian* (Clive Barret's) tarots, with other decks in various states of debordering. These days few of the Italian art decks stay in the pristine state in which they arrived (you know the ones I'm talking about: the decks with the name of each card in sixteen different languages; do I really need to know what "Ace of Cups" is in Swahili?). The Italians have a highly developed fine art approach to the cards (something about having tarot and fine art techniques as part of the background cultural landscape for several centuries breeds a certain easy familiarity that frees the imagination, I reckon), and they revel in "concept" decks, so I feel I'm doing the cards a favor in allowing them to stand unfettered by ugly white borders and an entire Berlitz manual of words.

By playing fast and loose with the cards once they're out of the box, I opened a whole new world for myself (not to mention entertaining myself for hours on end), but I am not alone. At any gathering of tarot enthusiasts, I am always struck by how the longer a person works with tarot the more ideas they get about what to do with it. We all know how tarot has inspired poetry, drama, dance, and art, but I am constantly impressed by how so-called "ordinary" people fashion ingenious bags and boxes, make stunning collages, and collaborate with others to create new decks—to name just a few of the directions the creativity surges. Once engaged, the creative impulse cannot be denied.

✦ A Headlong Rush

At some point long ago, perhaps with a vague idea that I might want to decoupage my entire apartment and all within it, I started accumulating piles of images from magazines, advertising, and just about every other paper source that crossed my path. They began to fill boxes when my bulletin board, refrigerator, scrapbooks, and journals overflowed. Something needed to be done. In an effort to get some handle on the rising tide, I started trying my hand at making collages ala the *Voyager Deck* (a splendid photo-collage deck created with scissors and glue in the misty days before PhotoShop). I began to use the images in a variety of ways, such as doing a relaxation exercise by letting the colorful pieces of paper guide me into making a tarot image. Another variation is to create a specific vision of a card (some of them are actually aesthetically palatable). When I'm feeling like procrastinating (more often that I would care to admit) I file the images into folders or envelopes that correspond to suits or specific cards. Much to my slightly astonished relief, I have discovered that it is a fun and stimulating exercise to sort through an album of "Strength" pictures or flip through a file of "Towers." Of course one could probably also paper the bathroom with an entire tarot tableau if one were sufficiently ambitious and enthused. There really is no stopping this sort of thing once it starts.

In my constant prodding of the imagistic and divinatory enve-lope, I found that I could even turn housecleaning into a divinatory exercise by gathering several bags or boxes and putting into them stray postcards (not to mention matchbooks and other small sou-venir type objects; at last! a use for that Hoover Dam refrigerator magnet and the tiny St. Louis Arch wall thermometer), crystals, stones, shells, and stray, single tarot cards. I pull out one of each object (one postcard, one shell, and one tarot card, for example) to create a reading. Hard to believe though it might be, I am very tarot centered, so I use the tarot card as a grounding point and weave the rest of the objects into what often turns out to be a remarkably coherent and fun reading (and as an extra bonus I have avoided tidying up for another day in the interest of tarot study and per-sonal life coaching). Sometimes I make a diorama or altarpiece out of the results. There are endless possibilities to this sort of process, and I have no doubt that more creative and inquisitive minds than mine can take this in new and clever directions.

The value of these kinds of exercises is in part due to their reliev-ing the pressure of modern life's relentless standardization (one size does not always fit all, dammit). By fostering creativity and personalization one gets an opportunity to deepen one's connec-tion to an already profound and powerful tool of wisdom and potential transformation. We do not have to merely accept what the world (or our local New Age bookstore) offers us—we can put our own unique stamp on our cards, and, through that, our lives. We are also afforded the simple satisfaction, far too often missing in modern life, of play and inventiveness (why should playing with art stop in grade school?). Working with the images, the cards, and the concepts of the tarot helps to confound lockstep conformity and opens up wellsprings of originality.

Go on, grab a pair of scissors!

Judgment

Deck Reviews

The Fey Tarot

reviewed by Diane Wilkes

Recent scientific studies have verified that there are two kinds of fairies—ones that are all sweetness and light and could easily be mistaken for angels, and ones who are fey creatures who contain all the light and dark qualities of human beings, along with some idiosyncratic traits all their own.

Okay, so I'm lying about the scientific studies. But in my travels, I have noticed that there is a divide. People who believe in fairies tend to categorize them into these two camps. The creatures that populate the *Fey Tarot* (ISBN 0-7387-0280-3) by Mara Aghem and Riccardo Minetti definitely fall into the second camp. Aghem, a renowned anime artist, brings her skills to bear on creating tarot denizens who are foolish and wise, saucy and shy, peaceful and spiteful, good and wicked. They're no angels, and they don't want to be, either.

The Fool card sets the tone with his self-absorbed adulation of a grinning pumpkin. Is he mentally unbalanced, or merely a quirky narcissist? Only the foolish know. The Magician card resembles a pale and idealistic Harry Potter in potions class at Hogwarts; the High Priestess could well be Hermione Granger, studying an old tome that holds the answers to all the questions. In fact, several of the cards would fit into the magical world of J. K. Rowling: the World card

0 The Fool

Il Matto
Le Fou

Der Narr
El Loco

The Fool from *The Fey Tarot*

could be Hogwarts, the Wisest (the Hermit in more traditional decks), with his white flowing beard, could play Dumbledore (though his phoenix has been transformed into a dragon), and the Devil card resembles the troll Harry and Ron brought down in the movie *Harry Potter and the Sorcerer's Stone*. Not only that, but one of the dreamier fey plays a dramatic game of chess in the Death card and the flying Tower is reminiscent of Ron's flying car. Even the Judgment card could be a post-examination scene from the Potter series.

I doubt these parallels are intentional: a magical world often possesses qualities and traits of other magical worlds. And the *Fey Tarot*, with its fantastical whimsy, allows the reader to enter a magical world indeed.

While this deck is not a variant of the more traditional *Rider-Waite-Smith Tarot*, anyone familiar with that deck should be able to read with the *Fey Tarot*. Strength is VIII, Justice XI (a new numbering for Lo Scarabeo). Most of the Major Arcana are traditionally titled, with the exception of "The Seer" for the High Priestess, "The Wisest" for the Hierophant, and "The Stars" for the Star.

The paranormal world of Aghem's fey creatures is continued in the Minor Arcana, where the suits are Wands, Chalices (Cups), Swords, and Pentacles. The Aces all display fairies that express their element—for example, the fey on the Ace of Chalices is doe-eyed and immersed in water. His hands cup water as he reaches out to offer you love in clear, liquid form. His limpid expression and his translucent wings are ever-so-soft and gentle.

But not all the fey are mild and temperate. In fact, some cards are more frightening in this deck than their *Rider-Waite-Smith* counterparts. The Nine of Swords, for example, shows a bright creature on her knees, penitent and afraid, as a large and sharp sword comes directly toward the small of her back, where she is most vulnerable. Minetti compares the dagger to the "Sword of Damocles" that hangs over all of us at one time or another. This fear made palpable is a frightening card indeed, though a gateway to the stars is only a few desperate crawls away.

The Two of Wands, which typically depicts individualism and independence, shows the shadow side of this card, displaying a fearful fey holding on to his nest with great trepidation. The fey, like many of us humans, aren't eager to grow up.

Not all the cards are so frightening, but they do lead us into an alien world. These are wee people—the fey on the Ten of Wands carries a huge burden, but it looks like an average-sized orange to us. These cards remind us of perspective, in more ways than one. Even a joyous card like the Ten of Chalices, which shows a happy couple ensconced in a jeweled and golden cup, doesn't look all that physically comfortable for those of us who are of slightly advanced years and/or don't practice yoga. And the large chalice is floating on water . . . how steady can that be?

The court cards are Knave, Knight, Queen, and King. While the King and Queen retain their traditional male and female forms, Knights and Knaves are gender diverse—hence the Knave of Chalices is a beautiful adolescent and the Knight of Wands, an impudent pixie. The artwork is incredibly engaging, never entering the overly cute and sweet zone that would mark these fey with the banal sign of the cherub. The colors are bright and rich and the characters that inhabit the cards equally so. The cards themselves are standard size, and the purple backs are reversible and set the mood for magic and mystery with a mirrored image. One querent described them as kaleidoscopic.

The book by Riccardo Minetti is both personal and wide ranging.

9   Swords

Spade   Schwerter
Épées   Espadas

The Nine of Swords from *The Fey Tarot*

The introduction focuses on the spiritually creative nature of the tarot. It includes black and white sketches of earlier incarnations of the cards, providing a window into the creative process that underpins the deck, as well as depicting the artist's approach. Minetti's role was to provide a tarot foundation for Aghem's fanciful artwork, and the book discusses this partnership in some detail.

An "Introduction to the Tarots" follows, which provides historical data, including a description of the three "iconographic" decks: the *Marseilles*, the *Rider-Waite-Smith*, and the *Thoth*. This information is illustrated with small sketches of the fey that have nothing to do with the actual information, which results in a charming, if disconcerting, display of material. This kind of factual information can often be boring or tremendously flawed—kudos to Minetti for presenting it in an unusually accessible and accurate manner.

The next section focuses on divination within the context of the *Fey Tarot*, but Minetti also expounds on the differences between the Major and Minor Arcana. The author is particularly poetic on the subject of the suits. However, Minetti devotes more space to the Major Arcana in both this section and in the card definitions, which are the main focus of the volume. The card definitions are unusually rich and nuanced for a companion book.

X   The Wheel

La Ruota   Das Rad
La Roue   La Rueda

The Wheel of Fortune from *The Fey Tarot*

The last section of the book is devoted to divinatory spreads, of which there are four. Some people find the English translation of the book from the original Italian to be problematic, lessening its readability, but I have a tendency to fall into the voice of the author, whether the idiom is Cajun, West Indian, or, in this case, less-than-flawless English as a second language. The book's format, however, does take a bit of getting used to, because the paragraphs aren't always separated by the standard amount of spaces.

The creatures of the *Fey Tarot* insisted on being a part of this review, determined to make their voices heard. I pulled a card to describe the essence of this deck and received the Wheel of Fortune. It is unique in that it shows two fey creatures creating their own wheel, as opposed to being the hapless respondents of the twists and turns of fate. They create this wheel from the fundamentals of life: tiny trees, houses, bridges. The essence of this deck is that of a different, magical, and slightly capricious world, a world that rewards audacity and creativity. It is a playful deck, a deck that has different rulerships and different rules.

I also selected a card for the secret key that will unlock the fey's mysteries: the Six of Pentacles, which shows an oversized, bountiful creature dripping with golden coinage that she creates and emits. These coins are part of her magic that she bequeaths to the less fortunate. The more you are willing to give of your time and effort, the more golden gifts of insight you will receive from the *Fey Tarot*. As both the Wheel and the Six of Pentacles show interactions with others, this is another message from the fey: read for others with this deck. These fey love to show off, and so they seek a wider public. Offer it to them, and you will likely receive greater gifts than you thought possible. And don't be fooled by its playful façade— the readings I have given and received from this deck have been both profound and layered. The humor makes the message palatable, but it's no fluffy Bertie Botts bean candy.

A Closer Look At:

The Shining Tribe Tarot

Created by Rachel Pollack

- 78 full-color cards and a 360-page illustrated book

- Cards are 4¾ x 2¾, with reversible backs and illustrated pips

- Combines the traditional archetypes of the tarot with a nature-based mythos: Wands, Cups, Swords, and Pentacles become Trees, Rivers, Birds, and Stones

- Artwork is inspired by tribal and prehistoric paintings and carvings from Africa, Australia, Europe, and the Americas

- Illustrated companion book includes Rachel Pollack's own poetry for each card

19 The Sun

3 The Empress

6 of Rivers

5 of Birds

10 of Trees

The Tarot of Prague

reviewed by Errol McLendon

My inability to draw a straight line has given me a special affinity for photo collage decks; however, there are special challenges to using this medium that are not always met by deck designers. Since the creators of a photo collage deck are usually working with whatever images they can find or put together, the meanings of the cards are often changed to fit whatever photos are available. In some decks, the meanings of the cards are retained, but the connection between the images and the meaning of the cards requires a great deal of imagination. With these challenges confronting them, Karen Mahony and Alex Ukolov, owners of a design studio in Prague, have put together a photo collage deck that not only honors the *Rider-Waite-Smith* imagery and meanings, but acts as a combination history lesson, art-appreciation class, and love letter to their home.

Even the box that contains the deck and book is beautiful. Through an intricately carved archway we find ourselves overlooking the breathtaking panorama of Prague's red tile rooftops, with domes and towers punctuating the landscape. The set itself contains a 300-page book that gives a crash course on everything you ever wanted to know about the city and the artwork that covers many of the exposed surfaces in Prague. The deck comes in a

DEATH

Death from *The Tarot of Prague*

small, three-sided portfolio tied with gold cord and signed and numbered by the creators. A small booklet is attached, but do not cheat yourself out of the immense pleasure of the larger accompanying volume. My only concern with the physical structure of the deck is that the cards are not laminated, which tends to make me question their durability for everyday use.

The brilliance of this deck lies in the parameters set by the visionary artists who created this tribute to their home. They used two-dimensional and three-dimensional art and architecture found all over Prague, but also supplemented these images with art from a 1940s Bohemian playing-card deck. Armed with these images, and some incredible computer manipulation, Ms. Mahony and Mr. Ukolov have created a tribute to the *Rider-Waite-Smith* imagery so similar to that classic deck that I was able to do a very accurate reading with the *Tarot of Prague* without having read a word of the accompanying material.

Since receiving this deck a week ago, I've found myself constantly flipping through it and enjoying the images. They are absolutely gorgeous. Every artistic genre is represented here, from medieval Gothic and Baroque traditions to Art Nouveau and Art Deco styles. There is also a wonderful dual use of imagery: main images in the foreground deliver one message, and lighter images making up the background deliver a more subliminal message. The deck also has a unique feature in that there are two Death cards. One card is very dark, and reminiscent of a Baroque

DEATH

Death from *The Tarot of Prague*

memento mori—a tableau created to remind the viewer that everyone is going to die. The other card is more closely related to the *Rider-Waite-Smith* image. This card uses puppets, as do several of the other cards, to make certain points concerning manipulation of people, events, and fate, and to honor the age-old Prague tradition of puppetry.

The Knight of Cups from *The Tarot of Prague*

The court cards are particularly easy to understand. Though the interpretation of these cards differs somewhat from my personal viewpoint, there is no questioning what these people are like when you look at the variety of characters depicted in the *Tarot of Prague*. Even the type of artistic style and historic period from which these images were gathered gives an in-depth picture of the energies of each court card, juxtaposing ancient art with modern techniques and sensibilities. I particularly like the absurdity of the Knight of Cups riding over the ancient city on an upside-down horse.

The accompanying book is a wonderful companion to this deck and also a very solid introductory tarot book. The end section on how to read cards packs all the essential information needed by a new reader into twenty-five pages, and even includes a new, very workable spread. The other element of great use to the beginning student is the way the Major Arcana cards are described. Every Major card is presented with both a short and long interpretation. Within the fuller interpretation of each card, the reader is given the history of the image along with interesting notes on some of the numerological and astrological correspondences of each card. It truly is a very complete beginning tarot course on the Major Arcana. I would have liked to have seen a bit more of this type of information for the Minor Arcana, but then the book would have had to expand to 600 pages. Don't get me wrong: the Minor Arcana also have short and fuller interpretations loaded with information. The book includes a small section on each of the cards that explains the source of the art and architecture used in the cards and where it may be found in Prague. There are also intriguing articles through-

■ out the book, explaining interesting historical and personal-interest
✱ stories related to the images on the cards.

■ More information on *The Tarot of Prague* (ISBN 0-9545007-0-9)
is available at www.tarotofprague.com, but don't go there unless
you're willing to be immediately entranced by this colorful, magical deck.

The Winged Spirit Tarot

reviewed by Elizabeth Hazel

I n the past ten years, U.S. Games has produced a growing number of theme-based tarots. While some of these products are
merely clones of the *Rider-Waite-Smith* patterns, some of the
newer releases like David Sexton's *Winged Spirit Tarot* and the
Connollys' *Feng Shui Tarot* present more original reworkings of the
seventy-eight card deck, showcased through superb artistic ren-
derings. Gaining release from slavish dependence on the *Rider-
Waite-Smith* requires considerable thought by the designer, which
is happily the case with the *Winged Spirit* deck.

The *Winged Spirit Tarot* (ISBN 1-57281-121-8) features a pan-
theon of angels for its theme. Sexton has drawn upon an eclectic
mix of angelic personalities to represent intermediary etheric
beings who convey messages, warnings, and inspiration from the
divine spirit to humanity. The primary source for the angel lore
used in this deck is Judeo-Christian literature, but the imagery
extends into Gnostic, Greek, and even Nordic myth for winged characters that embody the divinatory emphasis of the twenty-two Major
Arcana cards. As an example of this diversity, the Magician is portrayed as the biblical angel Metatron; the Empress as the Gnostic
mother spirit Sophia. A Valkyrie is used to represent the Chariot, and
the winged goddess of Greek origin, Nemesis, represents Justice.

Justice from *The Winged Spirit Tarot*

While hard-core angel fans may take issue with the inconsistency of David Sexton's choices for the Major Arcana, the deck overcomes this liability through the carefully designed and skillfully executed artwork.

The artist chose unique methods for presenting an internally unified deck. Characters are rendered on solid-color backgrounds. The lack of landscape features and distance perspective may strike some as denuding the deck of a vital source of visual cues often used for interpretation; however, it lends the deck an uncluttered and meditative quality similar to the Italian limited-issue deck *Le Mani Divinatorie*, which features hands positioned on a sky-blue background. Sexton takes full advantage of these featureless fields. Apropos of his angelic population, the winged beings on the Temperance card and the Queen of Cups hover in horizontal splendor, reveling in a weightless realm of light and air.

While the Major Arcana cards are backed with a neutral light gray, placing full attention on the angels chosen for the trump suit cards, the Minor Arcana's four suits follow a strict pattern of color and characterization, providing a beneficial tool for easy identification:

Wands: soft terra cotta background; figures colored in a palette of yellow, gold, rust brown, and red. The pip cards (Ace through Ten) feature a blond man with two fire sprites.

Cups: watery blue-violet background; figures colored in aqua, pink, lavender, and lilac. The pips feature a man and a woman accompanied by a cherub.

Swords: pastel teal background; figures colored in cool shades of gray and purple. The pips display a man and a harsh, dark angel.

Spheres (Pentacles): pale sage background; figures colored in a rich palette of golds, greens, brown, and chartreuse. The pips portray a woman with a solid and placid male angel.

This color scheme follows the elemental suit assignments of Wands to fire, Cups to water, Swords to air, and Spheres to earth.

The divinatory substance of the deck is solely reliant upon the figures drawn on each card, and this is where Sexton's talents come to the fore. The attitudes and poses of the characters are reminiscent of ballet and modern dance. As a choreographer meticulously designs a dance to tell a story without words, Sexton's angels and humans are posed in dramatic postures that convey the meanings intended for each card.

Strength from *The Winged Spirit Tarot*

In viewing the characters portrayed on the cards, the remarkable physical strength and flexibility of dancers like Nijinsky and Baryshnikov are brought to mind, as are the choreographic designs of Balanchine and Fosse. This quality is accentuated by the drawing style: Sexton's drawings are heir to the legacy of illustration artists like fin-de-siecle Swedish artist Kay Nielsen and early fantasy artist Frank Frazetta, whose styles were emulated and extended by contemporary action-cartoon and heavy-metal/goth artists. True to this line-intensive drawing technique, the figures are anatomically correct, but possess exaggerated muscular features: washboard abs and perfectly sculpted pecs and glutes. Sexton's drawings assure us poor humans, in our daily battles against gravity, that there are no drive-through burger joints or candy bars in the aetheric realm. This quality of perfect pumpitude has gained this deck the moniker of "the buff and studly tarot" on the Tarot-L list serve. Nevertheless, the internal cohesiveness of the suit cards is a bonus often neglected in theme decks. The court cards match by both suit and designation, and the Queens are exceptionally visually exciting. The four Aces should not be missed: each features a monochromatic rendering of the suit's symbol, with the Ace of Cups representing a particularly luminous achievement of design art.

The Queen of Spheres from *The Winged Spirit Tarot*

The *Winged Spirit Tarot* will appeal to those who enjoy cleanly

executed, uncluttered cards with beautifully colored figure drawings. Readers reliant on landscapes for visual cues may struggle in
their initial efforts to read this deck. Those who are offended by
explicit depictions of human anatomy should choose another deck.
But for those whose tastes include life-drawing and fantasy art, this
deck will delight the senses with its slick drawings and well-
planned presentations.

The Victoria Regina Tarot

reviewed by Diane Wilkes

My Aunt Sophia was the most elegant and fashionable woman I ever knew. Her entire wardrobe consisted of only black and white clothes. She clearly would have adored the *Victoria Regina Tarot*—a highly stylized, elegant black-and-white deck, designed by graphic artist Sarah Ovenall.

The deck, as its title implies, is based on the art and time period of the long and successful reign of Queen Victoria. Ovenall illustrates the deck with a seamless combination of Dover Art, photographs of the period, and copyright-free images. The result is seventy-eight works of art that are so compositionally sound that I've heard people describe them as not looking like collage at all.

Ovenall originally planned to design a set of playing cards, not a tarot deck. She was persuaded by her significant other, Georg Patterson (who coauthored the *Victoria Regina* companion book), that, as she was trying to create a symbolic system, she might as well design a tarot, since it provided a symbolic framework upon which she could build.

Modeling the *Victoria Regina Tarot* (ISBN 1-56718-531-2) on the popular *Rider-Waite-Smith Tarot*, Ovenall has created a deck that shares the spirit and message of that familiar deck, yet has created images that sparkle with a life of their own. The Fool carries a flower in one hand and a wand in the other, hip-hopping towards a precipice with great jauntiness. As in the *Rider-Waite-Smith*, a dog nips at the Fool's heels, but in this black-and-white deck, it's a British bulldog.

The English influence is also heavily present in the Lovers card, which depicts a gowned debutante at a ball. She is entering into the arms of one dashing beau while an equally elderly gentleman looks on the scene with dignified disapproval—or distinguished jealousy. The tableau is decorous and charming, a scene straight out of a Regency romance. I also like the fact that it's a woman who has to choose between two men, instead of the traditional man having the choice of two women.

While the deck isn't conspicuously feminist, it is based on a powerful woman, and some of the cards echo that female power in ways both subtle and overt. Not only does the Lovers card depict a woman with choice, but the Chariot has a woman at its bicycle helm and the Temperance card shows a beautiful woman creating an alchemical explosion by the light of the Moon—a very dynamic rendering of a card that can sometimes seem inert.

The cards are oversized, measuring approximately 3½ by 5½ inches. While I usually prefer smaller cards, the art on this deck demands (and receives) a larger setting. (How very queenlike of it!) The card backs contain a profile of Queen Victoria (who else?) in the center and are not reversible. The suits are Pens (Wands), Mason Jars (Cups), Guns (Swords), and Clocks (Pentacles).

1 ∘ The Magician

The Magician from *The Victoria Regina Tarot*

The suit choices are based on meaningful symbols. Ovenall transforms Wands to Pens because they are a "natural tool for an artist to express creative fire." Mason jars are, like Cups, vessels, and are also containers in which families preserve food, and, according to Ovenall, "indicate the changing nature of family life in the Victorian era." The element of water is equally changeable.

Ovenall selected Guns to repre- sent Swords in her deck as a tribute to Brian Williams, whose *Pomo Tarot* also made that switch. And if time is money, then pocket watches are a perfect currency exchange for coins. Additionally, the pocket watch represents the Victorians' passion for brisk efficiency and mechanical innovation.

Ovenall cleverly introduces and reinforces the familiarity of the symbols by integrating them into the art for the Major Arcana: on the table of the Magician sit a large pocket watch, a Mason jar, and gun, and the Magus grasps his Wand-Pen in hand. The Hermit's staff is also a pen.

Even though the suits are depicted with these nontraditional symbols,

Princess ∘ Swords

The Princess of Swords from *The Victoria Regina Tarot*

the cards themselves are titled Wands, Cups, Swords, and Coins. Coupled with the fact that the cards so closely resemble their *Rider-Waite-Smith* counterparts, no confusion should ensue. While my inclination is to see the Pen as representative of Swords, I never found Ovenall's assignments confusing.

Strength is VIII, Justice, XI. Card descriptions in the book don't specifically address reversals, but address the positive and negative range of each card. The court cards are, in this deck, often literally individuals in the court of Queen Victoria. Several of the male courts are different aspects of Victoria's spouse, Prince Albert, and Queen Victoria is pictured on each of the four Queens. She is also depicted as the Princess of Swords. This card is a bit disturbing. It evokes Jon-Benet Ramsey and makes me think—rather sadly— of young girls forced into an unnatural maturity. Other court cards include Oscar Wilde as the Prince of Wands (in this case, the pen is most fitting—though Wilde did wield his writing implement rather sharply and with acidic ink) and Prime Minister Benjamin Disraeli as the King of Wands.

The book includes an introduction and card interpretations, which contain a description, the actual interpretation, how each card plays out in your life, and notes on imagery sources. The book also includes three spreads designed exclusively for the *Victoria Regina Tarot*. One of them, Victoria's Chalice (designed by Comparative Tarot e-mail list owner Valerie Sim-Behi), also includes a sample reading with the *Victoria Regina Tarot*. Ovenall has included some material on creating a collage deck of your own, as well as an index, so you can look up which individuals correspond to which court cards and such.

I never think of the Victorian age as particularly diverse, so I was delighted to discover that this deck is somewhat multicultural. Quite a number of cards show individuals of African, Afghan, Japanese, and Javanese descent. The Seven of Wands, a card which depicts an embattled individual, takes on additional sociological meaning when the figure is a double minority.

A Victorian woman wouldn't appear in public without proper attire. I suppose that's why an elegant black velvet bag lined with dark blue silk comes with the set; you can dress your deck appropriately. A white box is also included for that purpose (a depressing sample of our less aesthetic modern society). However, the bag (with the cards) won't fit in the box, and the box won't fit in the bag, so the one you choose shows an implicit allegiance to a particular time period—the present or Victorian times. Also included are two extra cards that can serve as significators if you don't wish to remove any cards from a reading: the Magician and the Queen of Coins.

The 269-page *Victoria Regina Tarot Companion* has the appearance of a weighty and learned tome. This might inspire an initial concern that stultifying and dull history is what lies in wait on the pages, but if you can just bite the bullet and brave the first chapter, you will find an eminently readable book. It's a well-balanced combination of interesting Victorian factoids and fresh, appealing card interpretations. At the end of most of the card descriptions is a short "Notes on Sources" section, which offers additional humorous and/or ironic commentary that offers the reader additional insights into the time period.

The Chariot card provides a perfect example of this. The cyclist is originally from an illustration called "Emancipation," which accompanied

7 ∘ The Chariot

The Chariot from *The Victoria Regina Tarot*

an editorial decrying the moral laxity caused by increased women's rights. The essay complained that modern women cared more about freedom and fun than duty or family, and compared the young woman of 1892 highly unfavorably to her counterpart of a hundred years before. Her two ambitions are to have plenty of *oof*, no matter by what means, and to be as much like a man as it is possible for a woman to make herself.

Even the book is aesthetically pleasing. Some lovely images not found in the deck itself illustrate the chapter frontispieces; I love the one of Queen Victoria looking inscrutably at the *Victoria Regina Tarot* Empress card!

Sometimes theme decks are limited because of their subject matter, and only aficionados find them of much sustaining interest, but the *Victoria Regina Tarot* transcends its genre. The multilayered images offer a wealth of interpretational shadings, enabling the reader to utilize the book information in depth—or not at all. One could read with these cards without using the companion volume, but why would one, when the book is so enjoyable and worthwhile?

I recommend this set highly to tarot enthusiasts looking for an elegant and expressive deck that is similar enough to the *Rider-Waite-Smith* for immediate accessibility, yet different enough to offer the artistic eye a feast in black and white. The set, which contains not only a beautiful deck and a lengthy and well-written book, but also a well-crafted tarot bag, is a bargain . . . in more ways than one.

A Closer Look At:

The World Spirit Tarot

Illustrations by Lauren O'Leary
Text by Jessica Sczuka Godino and
Lauren O'Leary

- 78 full-color cards and a 192-page mini-book in a slip case

- Cards are 4¾ x 3¼, with nonreversible backs and illustrated pips

- Hand-colored linoleum block prints feature uniquely stylized, multicultural artwork based on the designs of Pamela Colman Smith and Lady Frieda Harris

- Court cards are replaced with "people" cards: Seer, Seeker, Sibyl, and Sage.

- Presents cards as a continuum of meaning, rather than polarized "upright" or "reversed" interpretations

Medieval Enchantment:

The Nigel Jackson Tarot

reviewed by Errol McLendon

I originally reviewed this deck in May of 2001 in Deni Richter's World Tarot Network online newsletter, and portions of that review are reprinted here with her permission. In that review, I looked at the deck mainly from an artistic perspective rather than a practical one, having read very little with the deck at that time. Since then, *Medieval Enchantment: The Nigel Jackson Tarot* has become the main deck I use when reading for other people. This new perspective of the deck demands that I republish and enhance my original review.

The artwork is the first element which attracted me to the deck, and I still love the world the deck has created. It is soft and inviting, part children's illustration, part medieval epic mural. The Temperance card on the box is only a hint of the beautiful illustrations contained in this unique deck.

The accompanying booklet (actually fairly large at 146 pages) gives very specific card meanings based on Pythagorean numerological concepts. The booklet gives a thumbnail sketch of the energy each number emits. There is also an interesting section which identifies the energies shared by the Major Arcana cards that reduce to the same base number. If you're not a master of Pythagorean numerology, please don't avoid this deck. The booklet tells you all

EIGHT OF STAVES

The Eight of Staves from *Medieval Enchantment: The Nigel Jackson Tarot*

you need to know and gives an excellent bibliography, but the cards definitely speak for themselves. I personally have not done any additional research in this area, and I continue to get excellent readings from the cards simply by allowing Nigel Jackson's beautifully rendered images to speak to me.

The main element I have grown to appreciate in the cards is the illustrator's choice to separate the pips from the card illustration in the Minor Arcana. The Minor cards are fully illustrated in the lower half of the card, but separated from the main illustration—usually in the heavens above—is a pip representation. This technique frees the artist to draw illustrations below the pips without being forced to include a sword, stave, cup, or coin in the scene. For example, the Seven of Swords is a picture of a fox trotting stealthily across a landscape to depict "evasive cunning," as seven swords appear in the sky above him. The Eight of Staves shows a shirtless young man carrying a scroll and running with a ribbon around his waist as if he has just crossed a finish line. Above him, floating in the air, are eight staves or arrows in a crosshatched pattern. The energy of the illustration vibrates with "speed."

The Major Arcana also shows a great deal of originality without straying so far afield that the cards are unidentifiable. The Magician has changed to the Juggler. The familiar posture of pointing to the heavens and to the earth is not present, but the Juggler glows with a spiritual light which gives the impression that he is divinely inspired. Popess and Pope replace the High Priestess and Hierophant. Strength becomes Fortitude, and is a particularly beautiful card. A lion wearing a garland of roses lies beside a kneeling woman, licking her hand as she pets him—a truly loving interpretation of strength born of love and trust.

The one challenge the deck presents for me is in the similarity between the court cards. The hair color, eye color, and skin tone on all the court cards are similar. Only the color of their garments is distinct: fiery red for Swords, earthly greens for Pentacles, intellectual yellow for Staves, and hints of emotional blue for Cups. This small obstacle, however, by no means takes away from the overall beauty and usefulness of the deck.

The cards are a bit larger than the standard deck size, which some people may not like, but I believe it was necessary in order to do justice to the intricate scenes created on the cards. They are well worth buying a larger storage box.

Medieval Enchantment: The Nigel Jackson Tarot deck and book (0-7387-0581-0) is published by Llewellyn Publications in St. Paul, Minnesota. Nigel Jackson has shown us what can be accomplished by honoring the age-old messages in the tarot while enveloping these messages in the style of a new visionary. The cards are ideal for readings, and exceptional for meditation and pathwork. Nigel Jackson has given the tarot community a brand new world of images to dive into and enjoy.

XI FORTITUDE

Strength from Medieval Enchantment: The Nigel Jackson Tarot

The World

Spreads

IL MONDO LE MONDE XXI THE WORLD EL MUNDO

DIE WELT DE WERELD

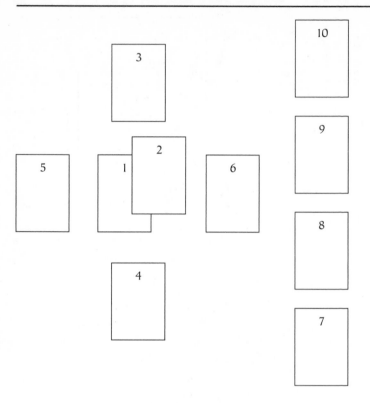

The Celtic Cross Spread

This is one of the most common and useful spreads for divining potential outcomes.

1. The querent
2. Influences on the querent
3. Message from higher self
4. Foundation of the question
5. The near future

6. The far future
7. The querent's fears
8. The querent's environment
9. The querent's hopes
10. The final outcome

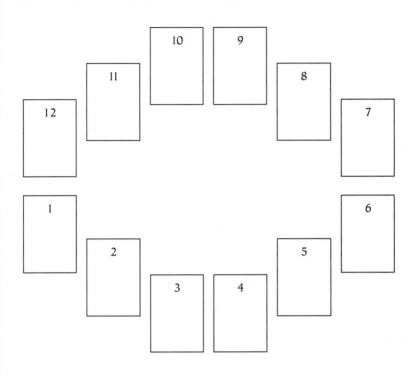

The Horoscope Spread

This spread uses the twelve houses of the horoscope chart. You can also look it as a "twelve-month" spread, each card representing a month of the year.

1. External self, persona
2. Personal resources, money
3. Communication
4. Home, security
5. Creativity, romance
6. Work, health

7. Partners, relationships
8. Power, sexuality
9. Travel, philosophy
10. Career
11. Friends, networks
12. Subconscious, dreams

—From *Designing Your Own Tarot Spreads* by Teresa Michelsen

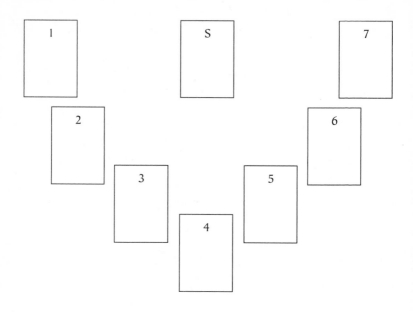

The Horseshoe Spread

This is a good spread for when you're facing an uncertain situation. Choose a significator card and place it at the center of the spread.

1. Past conditions

2. Querent's present situation

3. Future outlook

4. Best approach to the situation

5. The attitudes of others surrounding the querent

6. Challenges to be faced

7. The final outcome

—From *Legend: The Arthurian Tarot* by Anna-Marie Ferguson

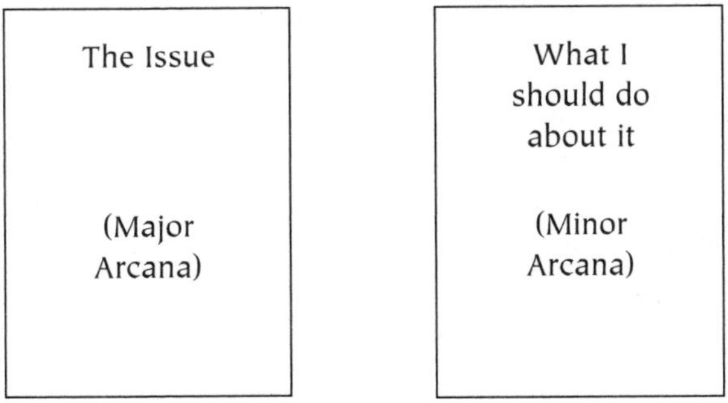
The Issue
(Major Arcana)
What I should do about it
(Minor Arcana)

The Snapshot Spread

This is a handy two-card spread for when you need focus or guidance for a problem. Divide the deck into the Major and Minor Arcanas and think of your problem. Choose a card at random from the Major Arcana stack; this is your "what" card—the issue facing you. Next choose a card at random from the Minor Arcana card; this is your "how" card—the best way for you to proceed.

—From *Heart of Tarot: An Intuitive Approach* by Amber K and Azrael Arynn K

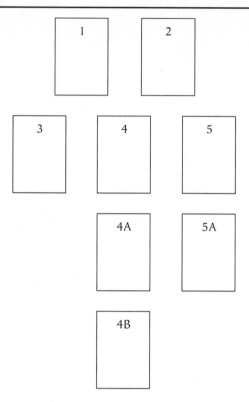

The Choices Spread

This spread is useful for times when you face a choice. First place two cards (1, 2) representing the question and the querent's position in the situation. Then split the deck into as many piles as you have choices, and from each pile take a card to represent the outcome of those choices (3, 4, 5). After studying each outcome, draw up to three additional cards for clarification as needed (4A, 4B, 5A).

—From *Heart of Tarot: An Intuitive Approach* by Amber K and Azrael Arynn K

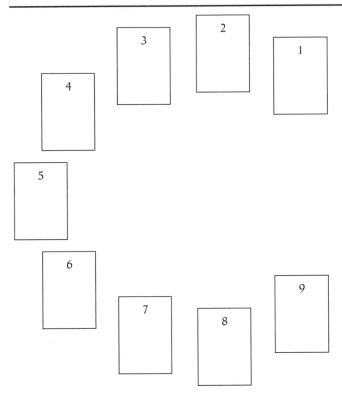

Dark Goddess Spread

When looking for guidance about your place in life and your future directions, try this spread, which invokes the energy of the dark Moon.

1. What needs protection
2. What needs patience
3. What needs acceptance
4. What needs release
5. An unconscious insight
6. A new perspective
7. What needs healing
8. Advice
9. Transformation/Outcome

—From *Tarot For All Seasons* by Christine Jette

✳ ☆ ✳ ☆ ✳ ☆ ✳ ☆ ✳ ☆ ✳ ☆ ✳ ☆ ✳

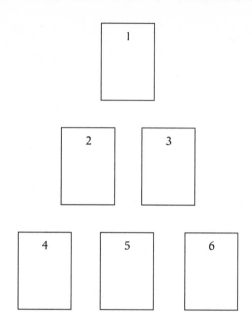

Pyramid of Consciousness Spread

This spread is for a more in-depth look at any issue or dream. It may reveal deeply hidden complexes and memories that affect your functioning in the present.

1. The core issue
2. Past
3. Present
4. What's hidden
5. What must change
6. Potential outcome

—From *Tarot & Dream Interpretation* by Julie Gillentine

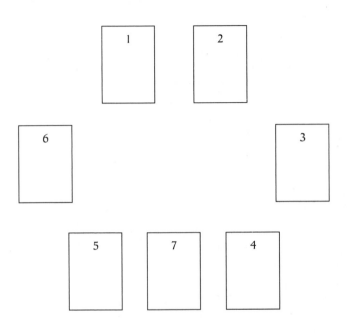

Career Spread

When you're looking to branch out into a new career or start a new endeavor, try this spread.

      1–3. Strengths that bring you to look for a new career

      4–5. Career ideas that draw on these strengths

      6. Any obstacles to pursuing a new career

      7. Any preparation needed first

—From *Designing Your Own Tarot Spreads* by Teresa Michelsen

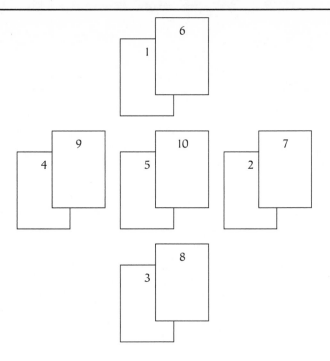

Elemental Cross Spread

To examine the elemental energies at work in your life, try this spread. Draw the first five cards, laying them facedown. Then draw the next five cards and lay them faceup on top of the first five. The faceup cards show the elemental energies involved in your question. Read these, then move them aside and turn over the cards underneath to show hidden influences. (1, 6 = Earth; 2, 7 = Air; 3, 8 = Fire; 4, 9 = Water; 5, 10 = Spirit.)

—From *Tarot for the Green Witch* by Ann Moura

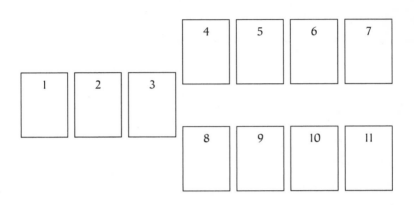

The Fork in the Road Spread

Here is another useful spread for determining the outcome of a choice.

1. Foundation of the issue

2. What led up to making this choice

3. The choice that has to be made

4–6. What will happen next if Choice A is made

7. Long-term outcome of Choice A

8–10. What will happen next if Choice B is made

11. Long-term outcome of Choice B

—From *Designing Your Own Tarot Spreads* by Teresa Michelsen

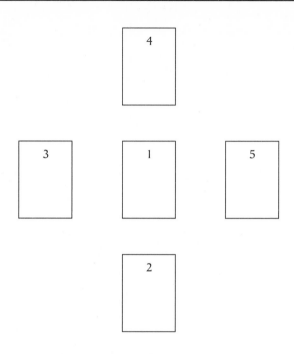

The Four Seasons Spread

The Four Seasons spread is suggested when timing issues are involved. If things seem blocked and at a standstill, this spread can reveal what needs to move.

1. The issue, the present
2. South, summer, incubation, what's hidden
3. West, fall, harvest, what must be released
4. North, winter, metamorphosis, what must be achieved
5. East, spring, emergence, what's coming into being

—From *Tarot & Dream Interpretation* by Julie Gillentine

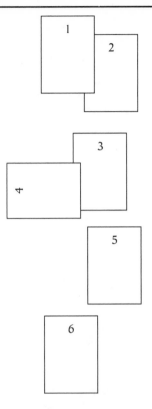

The Hanged Man Spread

Each card in this spread is read twice—first as an outer problem (upright meaning), and then as an inner response (reversed meaning).

1: **The Tree From Which He Hangs**
What am I depending on?

2: **The Rope That Ties Him**
What is hanging me up?

3: **The Conscious/Right Leg**
What have I assumed?

4. **The Unconscious/Left Leg**
My unconscious beliefs

5. **The Hidden Hands**
What am I sacrificing?

6. **The Illuminated Head**
The illuminating idea

—From *The Complete Book of Tarot Reversals*, by Mary K. Greer

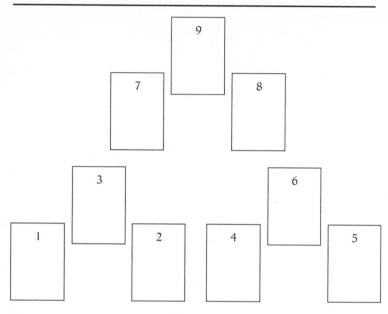

Internet Romance Spread

Online dating has recently become a popular topic for tarot readings. Use this spread to clarify some of the unknowns in the situation and gain advice about the next step.

    1. His or her impression of you from the Internet

    2. Your impression of him or her from the Internet

    3. The dynamics of your relationship on the Internet

    4. What he or she doesn't know about you

    5. What you don't know about him or her

    6. Your true compatibility

    7. Whether meeting in person is a good idea

    8. How the meeting may affect your relationship

    9. Overall advice in this situation

—From *Designing Your Own Tarot Spreads* by Teresa Michelsen

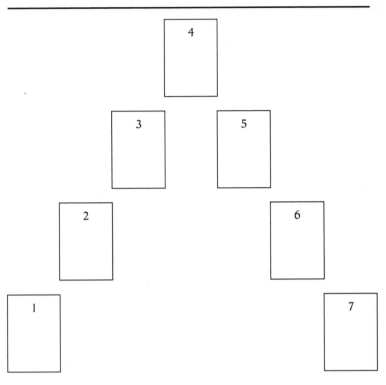

Mystic Pyramid

This spread is good for when something is bothering you, but you can't quite put your finger on it.

1. Past

2. Present

3. Near future

4. What's really on your mind

5. How others react

6. Obstacles or challenges

7. Likely outcome

—From *Tarot for the Green Witch* by Ann Moura

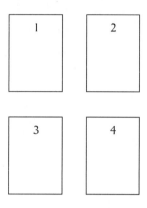

Crossroads Spread

Representing the four corners of a crossroads, this deceptively simple-looking spread is ideal for times when you feel a need for a new focus or change of direction.

1. What holds or binds you; what you can't see
2. What's offered in the moment; what you see
3. What will result if nothing changes
4. A new path, a different road, a new opportunity

—From *Tarot & Dream Interpretation* by Julie Gillentine

Notes

Notes

Notes

Notes

Notes

Notes